A Memoir by
Michael Philip Grove

Edited by Robert Grove

© Robert Grove 2008

All rights reserved. This book may not be reproduced in whole or in part, stored in a retrieval system or transmited in any form, except by reviewers for the Press, without written permission from the copyright holders or the publishers.

ISBN 978-0-9559200-0-4

Published by *Campden People*

Printed and bound in Great Britain by Vale Press Ltd, Willersey, England

CONTENTS

Foreword by Gerard Noel iv
Editor's Introduction by Robert Grove vii
Acknowledgements viii
Family History by Robert Grove ix
Chapter 1 - Early Years 1
Chapter 2 - World War 1 9
Chapter 3 - Into Action 17
Chapter 4 - Return Home 21
Chapter 5 - Return to the Armed Forces 25
Chapter 6 - Return to France for the second time 29
Chapter 7 - End of World War 1 33
Chapter 8 - Civilian Street once more 35
Chapter 9 - Chance of work improving..................................41
Chapter 10 - Beginning of World War 2 49
Chapter 11 - Back to England 57
Chapter 12 - Drafted Middle East 59
Chapter 13 - Period of Sickness 65
Chapter 14 - Back to my Unit 69
Chapter 15 - Aleppo Airfield and surrounding area 73
Chapter 16 - Movement to Iraq 75
Chapter 17 - A personal episode 70
Chapter 18 - Back with my Unit 83
Chapter 19 - Journey to Egypt 85
Chapter 20 - Back to work and a meeting with Churchill......87
Chapter 21 - Leave Egypt for The Dodecanese Islands.........95
Chapter 22 - War about over 108
Chapter 23 - Return Journey, England and Home 107
Chapter 24 - Settling back into Civilian Life 113
Appendix 123

FOREWORD
to
A Memoir by
Michael Philip Grove

by
Gerard Noel

I am delighted to write this Foreword to the excellent memoir by Michael Philip Grove.

I have long known his son Bob, along with his delightful wife Betty, while Bob's late brother Tony was a life-long friend.

The Grove's are an old and respected Campden family whose members have long made an important contribution to the life of our community.

Bob was a builder and the town possesses many monuments to his skill. These vividly written memories of his father afford a vivid insight into the life of Campden and its inhabitants revealing aspects of a period which would otherwise be forgotten. It is thus a valuable testimony.

His family, like my own, can trace its Campden roots back to the seventeenth century. The Grove's were builders even then, and as the author remarks, were responsible for many of 'our very fine structures'.

The Campden of the early twentieth century belongs to a different world. An almost complete absence of traffic was one feature, although Michael Grove recorded seeing the first motor car which came to Campden. This was in 1909 when King Edward VII drove through the town. He was cheered on all sides by Campdonians whose loyalty was not diminished by the fact that most of them had a harsh life, working hard for as little as sixpence an hour.

In that forgotten age, before the computer/television revolution, people made their own fun and were happy, despite the hardships.

The sense of fun echoes down to us in the nicknames of some of the Campdonians of that time. Michael Grove gives us some examples: 'Forty Merriman', 'Ninety Griffin', 'Fudger Yates', 'Jigger James', 'Nezzie Plested', and many more.

The absorbing narrative provided me with many happy memories of my own, by the mention of various characters I knew well myself. One was Laurence Ladbrook, at one time the town-crier, a role no longer existing (Seamus Stewart was the last).

Michael served gallantly in both wars, having falsified his age to be accepted into the army in World War 1. Life after being demobbed was not easy, but the conviviality of Campden helped to make it bearable. There were many more pubs than there are today and beer, cider and homemade wine were cheaper than tea.

I could go on indefinitely, but must resist the temptation. I will not delay any further in allowing you to plunge into these memoirs which I am sure you will read - as I did - with the greatest pleasure.

Gerard Noel
Campden
15.iii.MMVIII

> LOVE GILDS THE HOURS.
> UNFOLDS THE FLOWERS
> OF PASSING DAYS.
> WHERE LOVE IS ALL,
> NO SHADOWS FALL,
> THE SUNSHINE STAYS.
> M.P.G. 1962

Church Street looking south/west

EDITOR'S INTRODUCTION

When my father, Michael Philip Grove, was in his early to mid 70's, he asked for a typewriter and a pack of A4 plain paper.

I was aware that he was about to amuse himself during his latter years with some form of writing and with a typewriter, a machine that he had never operated before.

Typically, in his usual quiet manner, this new found occupation was not discussed and I being always frantically busy, now regretfully, did not enquire.

After he had passed away, his writings were discovered and which were laid out in the form of his memoirs.

Since then and with the passing of time, local books were being produced and although somewhat biased, I decided there was sufficient interest in my father's memoirs worthy of publication. Also, that it had taken place during a century of great changes and incredible advancement. Now in my own retirement, with less pressure on life and more time on my hands, I have decided to produce this, 'My Father's Memoirs'.

His writings scan only briefly over his childhood years, but portray the difficult and hard times as a teenager.

Following on, he illustrates his progression in masonry work and experiences at home and abroad, during both world wars.

He mentions little about his leisure time, although I understand he was once in a local hockey team and was also very fond of old time dancing.

Known for being both a quiet and personal man, rarely showing his feelings, there is, however, evidence of his innermost feeling of love and devotion to his wife, my mother, whose maiden name was Edith Benfield. He also had great attachment to his five grandchildren, Steven, Sara, Carol, Rachael and Amanda, whose company he enjoyed immensely.

There are around sixty or so place names mentioned in France, Belgium, The Middle East, The Dodecanese Islands and in this country during his time spent in both world wars.

ACKNOWLEDGEMENTS

I am deeply indebted to The Hon. Gerard Noel for producing a Forward for my father's memoir. In a way, I feel a strong association with Gerard's ancestral Campden Estate.
My Great Grandfather, John Sharpe, lived with his wife and family in a stone built thatched cottage adjacent to the church. It is therefore fair to assume that he was employed on the estate to whom the cottage belonged. My Great Aunt, John Sharpe's daughter, lived in the same cottage until it was demolished in the late 1950's.
My Godfather, Tom Randall, was gardener on the estate around the 1930's/1940's period and lived in a bungalow in the grounds of The Court House.
I, myself, used the Court Barn and surrounding area for some 30 plus years whilst operating a building business.

My thanks to Judith Ellis for assistance and advice with the book layout. To Jill Wilson for proof reading and advice. To the Chipping Campden Family History Group for their support and assistance with the book 'launch'. To my daughter, Amanda, for sorting me out on numerous occasions when I became stuck on the computer.

NOTE TO READER

As little as possible has been changed of the text my father wrote, leaving his phrasing, much of his punctuation and even the occasional typo unaltered.
Modern place-names have been added in square brackets [ ] in some cases.

Robert Grove May 2008

FAMILY HISTORY

Michael's parents were Thomas and Lily Grove and they lived in 2 Church Cottages, which was a small stone built thatched cottage. Charlie Withers, the blacksmith, lived two doors away. There was a pump at the front, which served the whole row of cottages.

Michael was the second of eleven children, their names and dates of birth were William George born 1897, Michael Philip 1899, Robert Thomas 1903, Herbert Charles 1905, Eleanor Mary 1909, Edward Frank 1912, Margaret Ann 1915.

His mother's maiden name was Lily Sharpe, she was one of ten children born to John and Sara Sharpe who lived in a stone built thatched cottage which belonged to the Gainsborough Estate. The cottage used to stand near to St James Church on the piece of land between the South Lodge and Court Barn, now cordoned off with bollards and chain link.

Church Cottages

Aunt Agnes, Lily's sister, was still living there on her own until 1956, when she had to move out because the cottage was to be demolished. The cottage still had its outside earth closet in use. She moved in with one of her sisters Mrs Scott, who lived in No 12 Almshouse, which was at the rear and nearest to the Eight Bells. No's 11 & 12 shared a communal staircase.

John & Sara Sharpe

ix

Agnes was married to Thomas Kilby Keely who was a Lance Sergt in the Gloucester Regt. They had only been married a short time when his Regiment was sent over to France during World War One. He was unfortunately killed in action on 19th August 1917 aged 29 years. He is buried in the New Irish Farm Cemetery, Ypres, Belgium.

Thomas and Agnes taken about the time of their marriage

The following is a copy of a letter sent to her by his Army Captain:

"It is with very deep regret that I have to inform you that your husband, Sergt Keely, was killed in action on the 19th inst. He was a hero to the end and met his death while advancing on a German position. He was a great fellow, loved and esteemed by all his officers and men. To me, his loss is very great indeed. I shall never forget the excellent work he did for me at all times. Please accept my deepest sympathy in your very deep sorrow."

After their return from WWI, Michael and his two brothers set up in business as Grove Bros. Ironically, Grove Bros. Builders were awarded the job to demolish the old cottage and clear the site.

Church Street
Old Cottage on right hand side

x

The stone was bought by Leo Reynolds and it was used to build two semi-detached houses in Grevel Lane: one for himself and one for his parents. At that time, Leo Reynolds was working at the Council Offices, Moreton in Marsh, as a Building Regs. Inspector.

Michael Grove's family trade 'stonemasons' can be traced back nigh on two hundred years, with the skills handed on from father to son. His great grandfather, Michael Grove, was 43 years of age in the 1841 census, living in Leyesbourne, then spelt 'Lazeborn', occupation listed as stonemason. The trade being carried on through the years to himself. There are receipts for building work carried out by his grandfather, Michael Grove, in 1866 for Nathon Izod and in 1875 for James Horne.

Robert Grove

Old receipts

High Street, Chipping Campden

The life of a Country Lad

A Memoir by
Michael Philip Grove

Chapter One
Early Years

It is very rare, or ever, that one hears or reads a memoir of an ordinary working man. So I thought I would endeavour to write my own. I am aware that it will be very sketchy, and will over run itself at times. Times and incidents will criss-cross, but generally, the story will be correct.

This memoir will begin at about 1910. The earlier years are always very vague. I was born in Chipping Campden on October 13th, 1899 and at this time of writing it is 1974.

As far as it was possible, I traced my ancestors as far back as a burial in 1703. So we were existing in this town in the 1600's, but, as so very few people could write or read at that time, names became mis-spelt and confused and not really legible. I think our name then may have been spelt Gruff.

I think that most certainly my ancestors were involved in the building of our very fine structures, for trades were normally passed from father to son. I have in my possession, a beech mallet, which has seen a lot of service over many years, could be several generations, as these old boys took great care of their tools in the old days. This mallet served me well, all through my stone working career. Until in the end I split it, through being careless, and using a small headed chisel while cutting a large stone, instead of a mallet headed chisel. It is obvious by this time, that I finally followed the trade of my forefathers.

Now back to about 1909. Round about this time, I saw the first motor car, which came to Campden. Col. Staunton at the Court House and Dr. Dewhurst, at Ardley House (now Kings Arms Hotel). Then the King, Edward VII came through in a car. We were all in the street to see this very rare sight. Also, about this time, 1910, "Bleriot" a Frenchman, was the first to fly the channel, and from this, I saw the first aeroplane. Of course we had the railways and canals, but now, we are seeing the beginning of great changes. People used to say "Pigs might fly!" if something difficult was asked, for no one dreamt of the great changes which were about to take place.

At that time, the roads were made of broken blue stone, and rolled in by steam roller. These weighed about 10-12 tons, the roadmen used to dig loam and soil from the road side and sprinkle on the stone to blind and bind it, then wetted by water cart, and rolled in. The stone was put in large heaps on the road side, and the old stone breakers spent weeks and weeks, breaking it to useful size, they wore gauze goggles for protection. All this was great fun for us, seeing the men at work, and especially the roller.

About this time, 1910, I saw Halley's Comet. It was quite a sight, with its very long tail. It passed over from east to west, quite high up in the northern half of the sky. It will be seen again in 1986. Life was pretty tough during these and the following years. There was very little work about, mostly estate work or farm repairs and sometimes a job at one of the big houses round about.

Most people walked to their work. They had to be there at start time, anything up to three or four miles each way, doing 10-12 hours each day for 6 pence an hour or less, in fact in 1912 the top rate of pay for tradesmen, was 6 pence an hour. So the labourer had much less.

In those days most workers had pieces of land, anything up to an acre, which they worked on when out of work or in spare time. They grew almost all their own vegetables, so much corn for bread, and other things like broad beans for market etc. They nearly all had a pig to feed up, to kill for home meat through the winter. I know, I used to love a slab off a ham fried for Sunday breakfast. I am the second of seven children, and we all had jobs to do, when we were old enough, before and after school.

It seemed to be my fate to receive a stroke with the cane across my back every evening when father came home from work, sometimes I deserved it, but however it became a regular feature.

My first school was the boys' school held at the church rooms, There is a photo taken in the front yard. I am second from the left rear row. Headmaster was Mr Dewey.

The boy second from right in the third row was Bill Payne from Ebrington, he worked as a plumber in adult life and was always playing practical jokes. He eventually played Ned Larkin in the radio show "The Archers".

Boys at the C.of E. school (now the Church Rooms) c.1908
Michael is on the back row, second from left

I went to the Grammar School when I was still not eleven years old, through the scholarship exams. At that time I was in the very top seat at the elementary school.

At that time, the Grammar School was a very good and important place. There were lots of boarders, boys and girls, and day boys, all paid for, and, as one would expect, the scholarship pupils were looked down on. We were the poor and low class. I found it hard, not being able to have the best of books, and sports gear. Parents needed all the money they could get to buy the necessary things of life.

My first introduction to stone was in 1912 when I was twelve years old. I had had an appendix operation, and in those days a great thing was made of convalescence.

I was a schoolboy at the Grammar School in the High Street, and was not allowed to do anything or even go to school for some time.

At this same time my father was in charge of a rather large alteration at the Cotswold House Hotel so I spent a good deal of time there and had my first tuition in stone cutting.

Now back to school and no further stonework until after World War 1.

As for school sports or what have you, we only had Wednesday afternoons, from three o'clock, for hockey, or football, and cricket etc. and only then, if weather was fine. Hockey and cricket took place in "flag close" (now built up) and football was played at the far end of Pool Meadow. It took half of our time going there and back. Mr Osborne was the Head of the school then. He took Latin and History, Mr Davis, Science and Maths, and Mrs Duncan, French. Matthew Cox came next as Headmaster (from Wells) he brought more boarders. Three of them were South American. They were permanent boarders, their parents were very rich. Matthew Cox was very, very strict, but good and fair. It's a pity there aren't teachers like him today, around these years.

There was very little traffic on the roads, just an occasional horse-drawn carriage, or farm cart or wagon, or horses, but most regular of all, was the Station horse-drawn bus, which went to the railway station to meet all trains, taking passengers and parcels. I always remember "Ben the Busman" (Benfield). There was also a horse and trolley for goods delivery etc. At the monthly market, the square was full of penned sheep (pens being made of wooden hurdles) and cattle and pigs in the saleyard at the back of the Noel Arms Hotel. These were driven through the street to their destination, and lots were driven to the railway where they were loaded into trucks and taken by rail to Birmingham and elsewhere.

The street lighting at that time was by gas. Open flame in the lamp top with an off/on pull chain and the lamp lighter with his pole and lamp top arrangement, had to visit each lamp to light it, and later to put it out. This was done according to daylight hours, winter say 6pm to 10pm and not at all for three days about full moon. So very different to today. In the home it was nearly all oil lamps or candles. A few big houses had gas lights. (Gas mantles came later giving a better light). Cooking was done in the old fashioned hob grate, and all water boiled in a kettle over the fire. There were no hot water systems in cottages then or proper baths and WC's (these were earth-closets in a shed across the yard) and had to be emptied by hand into an ash ring, these later mixed up and carted away. You all were "primitive" even in those days, and if you wanted to find your way at night you had a candle in a made up lamp (first it was horn, then later glass in the lamp frame) or a hurricane lamp. These were the best then, they burnt paraffin, with a wick, to turn up or down. Bicycles had oil lamps, not paraffin and later acetylene which gave a very good light. Horse-drawn carriages had first, candles in lamps and later oil. By the way, riding was rough then, those blue stone roads were bad enough but all the by-roads were made of white local stone and in the summer it was clouds of dust and in wet weather well you can imagine the mess. Roadmen had a certain amount of road to look after. They had to scrape the mud off, and shovel it away, also all the grass verges had to be cut and trimmed up.

In those days too, nearly all water was obtained from wells, usually one well to a row of houses. There was a water supply piped from the reservoir in Conduit hill, this only went to the larger houses. A private supply from Conduit Hill supplied the Court House and Alms houses. (One tap here for the twelve houses) I suppose it was the supply for the Manor House in the old days. It is a lead pipe.

As for our amusements we usually had to make our own. In the summer it was mostly marbles, hoops, (these were iron, blacksmith made), some rough cricket, etc., and we spent a good deal of spare time, down by Haydon's Mill and the Brook by Juliana's Gate. (Good place for minnows). There was also a team game called Two, Four, Six, Eight, Ten. Four, five, or six boys on a side. This was a kind of leap frog. One side formed a bent chain held together and the others had to leap on. If anyone fell off, that side lost, and if the chain broke down that was a loss. They usually leant against a wall. In the winter one of the games was "Tippy-Tippy show the light", like Hare and Hounds but the hare carried a hooded lamp and had to flash it if the hounds called (Tippy) as above. Good exercise if it was dry. There was also "Tip Cat" and "Tig Tag Toe".

Water House, Conduit Hill
Photo taken by kind permission of the owner

I used to read a good deal and was able, a bit later on, to fix up a small electric light, then followed later by a cat's-whisker wireless with headphones. Messages were sent by Morse Code Telegraphy.

One of the star attractions for us youngsters was the steam cultivator. Two large traction engines one each side of a field and a large scuffle drawn back and forth over the field, worked by the large drum and long cable fitted under each engine. They also had a large living van, for when they were working away from home, (as did the steam roller people). In early summer this outfit used to come up the track, behind where I lived and into the Church field called Parsons Close. There they used to do repairs and maintenance on their equipment, and would use Withers the Blacksmith who lived nearby.

When these engines were travelling on the road, a man had to walk in front carrying a red flag. This of course was to warn people with horses. They made quite a noise, with their big heavy wheels and the steam would frighten any horse. Of course we used to play round these engines, when the coast was clear.

I was just thinking now how old Joe Court used to collect the ashes etc each week, with a couple of boys and an old horse and trolley. The tip was on the left, up Conduit Hill, but lots of it was taken and spread on the farm track in "Big Ground" (now Brodie's Way). Of course, there was none of the packages and cans etc, like the present time and not a great lot of ashes either. The wastage now in this modern age is tremendous as is the cost of its disposal. It's what they call progress, or the result of it.

Some of the roads are now covered with tarmacadam. This makes a cleaner road, also smooth to travel on, it's now ideal for bicycles. The new "Hercules" cycle could be bought for about three pounds fifteen shillings at this time.

Harold Pyment   Lord Campden

Territorials marching off to Campden Railway Station WW1

Photo: CADHAS

Chapter Two
World War 1

Now there are rumours of war. It seems that Germany is out for expanding. Anyway there are various treaties with other countries and through a Crown Prince in the Balkans getting assassinated we are finally forced to go to war with Germany. They are very powerful, and it takes several years before coming to an end. This affair began in August 1914 and I saw the local Territorials march off to the railway station on a Sunday, on their way to join the war effort.

Of course I was still at school then, but decided that my folks could not afford to keep me at school now we were at war. The school authorities made a big do about it, saying I was to sit for Oxford next season, but I was stubborn then and flatly refused to go back.

I did odd jobs about the town for a while, but was very unsettled. In the end I found myself a job in Evesham and lodged there in Albert Road and cycled home Wednesday, half day closing and on Sunday.

I was riding father's bicycle at the time, and thought that I would see how far I could ride up Aston Hill. I held firmly on the handlebars for leverage, but to my horror one side of the handlebar bent upwards, I thought that's torn it, I shall be for it now. Sure enough dad came out with the cane, and as he held it above me before he could strike, I reached up grabbed the cane and broke it over my knee, and said that's the last time you will ever strike me.

I became a counter jumper at the International Stores. The shop there was where the MEB showroom is now, near the "Cross Keys". We used to spend all day Monday weighing and wrapping sugar in one, two, four and six pounds. We used several two cwt sacks of granulated and some Demerara. I was also responsible for care of the cheeses, they came in about 28lb rolls wrapped in what was called mutton gauze.

Then there was a continuous job making up orders as well as serving in the shop. In those days there was a daily delivery all round the villages, by horse drawn van, no motor vehicles in those days. They used to deliver to Campden also. The order man had a regular job going out every day collecting orders. The shop was open till six pm daily and eight on Saturday. I have stood outside one open shop window, Saturday evenings, selling picnic hams at sixpence a lb. I can hardly imagine it now.

One Monday morning, my friend in the shop said he was going to join the army. So I went with him. I was only fifteen at the time. I went in with him and the recruiting sergeant looked at me and said "what about you?" I said I was not old enough and then he said "you are a big fine chap. Go outside and think about it." I did this, and soon went back in and joined saying I was nineteen. This was early 1915, my brother Bill had already joined the Navy.

Bill Grove aged 18, in Navy uniform (left) with brother Michael, aged 15, 1st Worcestershire Regt. 1915

We were sent to "Norton Barracks, Worcestershire" where I passed A1. The other chap was C3. Home Service only". Anyhow we were sent to the Worcs Training Depot, at Devonport, South Raglan Barracks where we were put through it, in a squad of about sixty. (I had been in the Boys Brigade at home, and went to camp with them, at "Rednal Hall" near Oswestry, Shropshire. The Rev. Jackson, vicar of Campden, arranged this. He had a brother with a big estate, which made it easier for us. We would never have been able to go otherwise, as no money was available. We had good military training under Harry Ellis and Tom Ellison and we had a good bugle band too.) (Oh yes, it was very good training, and discipline. It did us all good.)

This Brigade training made it easy for me, as I knew all the drill. We were six weeks altogether on the parade ground, then we went to Fort Tregantle for range firing. There we were in tents and the weather was beautiful. I was a very good shot and finished with a very high score. After this we did a bit of field work, also night operations, on the Brickfields, near the Barracks. In this I had to carry a 56lb box of biscuits, keeping just behind the line of troops. Each time a Verey light was fired everyone dropped flat and kept still, until the light went out, then off again. We were in full marching order and I had to put my box of biscuits down and get behind it each time the light went up. After a time that box felt like half a ton, heavier each time I picked it up. However I made it but was glad when it was all over. We used to march up Crown Hill for bomb throwing etc on the Moors. I remember we had a weird catapult affair, to send bombs a distance away.

The only others, were what were called Jam Tin Bombs, with a fuse which we lit and threw over arm. These things were quite a menace. Now our time has come. We are drafted to France. We get seven days embarkation leave, then parade outside the Gym at three thirty a.m. ready to go, in full marching order.

11

They give us breakfast in the gym, two mackerel each.

The Band finally, after "General Inspection", marches us off to the railway where we leave at six thirty for Southampton where we go on board for our journey to Le Havre (France). On arrival there, we had quite a march to the camp where we were put sixteen to a tent. This was terrible; also it was wet weather at the time. How the hell we managed I really don't know. What a mess we were in.

However, after a few days we were put on trains and sent up the line, often we were shoved in a siding for a time, to let something else through. When we finally arrive at the rail head about thirty six hours later, we have to march towards that part of the line, which is occupied by the Battalion I am going to join. That night we stop at a farm, and are put in a barn, half full of straw. Nice to be on straw but there were candles burning everywhere, it's a wonder the place was not set on fire. These farms are set up in a kind of square, house one side, barns another side, stables and cow sheds the other, with the muck yard in the middle. There was a brick wall all round about 5ft 6ins high, and the usual water pump. This we found chained and locked in the morning, so you can imagine how we felt when we wanted a wash and brew up. Had a fine go at the farmer. He let us have water for tea but that was all. We now got ready to move again, loaded like camels and moved on towards where our battalion would be.

We finally arrived late evening, the Battalion coming in from the front soon after, and for a few days rest. This was when I first tasted rum. The cooks had put the rum issue in the tea. We were allocated to the various parts of the unit and I was now able to give an address to my letters home. I am now No. 23611 Pte. M.P. Grove, No.8 Platoon 16 section B.Coy, 1st Battalion Worcestershire Regt. BEF, France. We are now on real active service. It was a very rough and tough existence. There were these long marches of anything up to, and from ten to eighteen kilometres (a kilometre is 1200 yards) and, as its now coming up to winter time, it's trench warfare. All through this we had to carry everything we possessed, also greatcoat, fur coat, mackintosh cape and ground sheet and with our rifles each had two hundred and fifty rounds of ammunition to carry. There were five pouches on each breast of our equipment, each holding three clips of five rounds and two bandoliers of fifty each. Slung crossways over our shoulders, you can imagine what a load this was. Also my section carried a box periscope and cooking dixie, to add to the load. Usually my section was put in front of my platoon on the march as we used to sing a good bit. This used to help us along, although on one occasion when we were relieved I had no recollection of the march back. So tired I marched automatically you see.

In the bad weather it was all mud and filth, dirty water in shell holes. Clothes and boots and equipment stayed on all the time while in the trenches. Only packs etc taken off and put in "dugouts" no washing either. I remember once, the day we were being relieved, eight of us washed and shaved in a mess tin of water. We rubbed the shaving brush round our face and neck after shaving. How we stuck it I will never know, we used to be in the trench for a week to a fortnight at a time, and very little sleep. I remember once, finding I had been asleep, standing on the firestep leaning against the parapet.

I had previously been making sightings with sticks on German machine gun positions. I found some forked sticks and straight pieces. I stuck one in front, put the straight stick in the fork and held the back end in the back fork. Then, when the Germans opened up his machine gun I sighted along the straight stick on to the flashes of his gun, and then pressed the back fork into the ground. There was time to do this while his shots worked round in an arc. When you got used to it you could tell by the sound of the bullets smashing into the parapet. I just ducked until they went by. Then I made a final check on the sighting. I had done two or three of these. Then at "Stand to", just before dawn it was reported to the Platoon Officer who arranged for those points to be strapped during the day.

There was, at this time, foot inspection every morning just after "stand to". Battalion doctor came round just after daybreak and looked at everyone's feet. In the worst of the weather one or two men were carried out quite often with what was called "trench feet". I was carried one morning. Doc said, "You will go out tomorrow". But luckily we were relieved that evening. I suppose the exercise of marching out and back to the rest billets saved my toes, although I had a bit of trouble with my big toes. I was regularly digging out what I call dead flesh from under my nails for a long time after this.

I should have said before this that we were all as lousy as cuckoos. There was no escape from it while we were living this kind of life. When there was a chance and Gerry was quiet we took off our shirts and ran a lighted match up the seams to kill lice and eggs. (Only those who actually experienced this life could possibly know what it was like). We washed and cleaned up as best we could when out on rest. We once only in my time were marched to a big bath laundry place. (Actually it was a brewery converted). There were big barrels cut in half, in which three chaps went in each half barrel at a time to wash down. That part was all right, but you had to dry and dress in this big open building. Hand in your dirty stuff and get clean in exchange. But these exchange clothes were as bad, or worse, than the ones you gave in. I tried to find my own old stuff, but was unlucky, too many there.

Another time we came out late from the line, I suppose it would be eleven o'clock before we could lie down and we were ordered to parade cleaned up for inspection at 9.00 a.m. All we could do was scrape the mud off the bottom of one's greatcoat and off the puttees and boots, and look over the rifle (which was our best friend anyway).

Once we arrived back out of the line at ten thirty p.m. and at two thirty were lined up, pick, shovel each man in turn, then march back up the line, trench digging till after daylight. Then march back again. Of course discipline was tremendous in those days. I don't for one moment believe that the modern youth would stick it. In any case everything is very different today.

At this time we were round about Ypres. There was a big salient there, and we marched through Ypres on our way into the front lines, at that time the famous "Cloth Hall" was undamaged, or very little. (When we passed through here near the end of the war the place was a shambles, all smashed up). Poperinge [*Poperinghe*] was near, we could see it easily, when we were out on rest. This was where "Tubby Clayton," Padre to the forces later founded "Toc H" meaning "Talbot House" in Poperinge .

There were lots of places round about that I still remember the name of. Paschendalle [*Passchendaele*], forward and to the right in front of Ypres on the Menin Road (what a hell hole). Then there was Elverdinge, Vlamertinge, Zonnebeke, and Fleury. Oh and we had "Hell fire corner" Ploegsteert and others where you nipped by pretty sharpish.

The town of Lille was some distance on our right about thirty miles as the crow flies. Malbrouck was behind, some distance away. We once came out of the line and my company were billeted in a big barn with straw to lie down on. This we thought was great. But in the morning we found ourselves covered with snow. We could see through the roof. Half the slates were off and here we had to break the ice on a pond to get a wash.

Now we have been ordered further down the line to relieve the French. A sort of flying squad. We had just about forty miles to march and finally arrived at Bruay. They put us in an old monastery; it was all made up for the French. Three tier bunks – we stayed a few days here and one day one or two of us went up on to some high level ground. A sort of common. There was a coal mine there that we wanted to see. It was a bit misty and while we were there, a small Bristol fighter plane landed near us, he had lost his bearing. We told him where we were and then held on to his wings while he revved up his engine for take-off. We used to see a lot of aerial combat, you could see every move and I saw many go down one time and another

Chapter Three
Into Action

Now, we are going into the line. This time my company was to be second line reserve to the Battalion and my section was officers' baggage party. Never will I forget it. It was the longest communication trench and the deepest and narrowest, that I ever went up. It seemed endless. Our baggage was in big, clumsy bags, and after a bit, we could not drag them along. The trench was too narrow so we climbed on top and went that way. We made a lot of noise and Gerry heard us and strafed us a bit. Still, we made it, and then had to go back to the road, for our own equipment etc. and back up this awful trench again. My word, what a dirty lot the French were. Filth of every description and their cooking boilers were left with stew tack in, nothing cleaned up.

It is now early March 1916, and this beautiful morning a party of us have to carry boxes of ammunition and Mills bombs up into the front line. In one place we go over a hollow place in the area. We could all see the small town of Souchez well behind the German lines, (this is in the Lens district) and it was obvious Gerry could see us. We were two to a box, carrying the ammunition up, and when we returned past this open space he gave us some hammer. Strafed us with light shells, we called "Pip Squeak". We ran for our lives, and when we dropped out of sight, I went down to get a drink out of the shell holes, oh dear there were bits of arms and legs sticking out. It appears the French had been pulled down over lots of dead from a previous battle, nearly made me sick. Another time we were strafed all day by "mini wafers" aerial torpedoes we called them. By carefully watching you could spot them coming and dodge out of the way, up or down the trench. At six o'clock in the evening we were ordcrcd up one way out of this area. They put fifty machine guns in that night, so they expected a raid. But it did not come to anything. I remember a "Cpl. Orgles". He came out forgetting his rifle and sent me back to get it for him. He ought to have been shot for it. Good job for him he was not found out.

I must go back a bit in time now, as on Feb 15th 1916 I got nicked by a Gerry bullet. It entered just under the two vent holes in my cap, left hand side and burst the wire grommet in the centre of the back. I was told, another quarter of an inch and that would have been my lot. I should explain here that our head-gear was the peaked hat, with a wire grommet inside the rim of the cap. For winter time we had waterproof cap covers. I kept my cap as it showed where the bullet entered and with a larger ragged hole at the back where the bullet passed out, after breaking the wire grommet. My mother kept it and I know she still had it in the nineteen fifties, but it got lost after she passed on. I should have included that at this time the first steel helmets were beginning to be sent to us. I saw the first four come to my company. I did not have one; in fact we all tried to avoid them for we found they felt heavy to wear. Also we did not have proper gas respirators then, only a woollen hood with eye pieces. These things stunk to high heaven with chemicals. Gas then was in cylinders, which were opened when the wind was in the right direction.

We used to have what was a "Green" envelope, once a fortnight, with which we could seal down a letter. This was supposed not to be censored; otherwise all mail was left open to be examined. Now in one of these green ones I told Mother about this bullet, but said not to say anything about it, to the local military, as it could get me into trouble, for making a false statement of age on enlistment. However she went to Colonel Staunton at the Court House, and showed him my letter and also she showed my birth certificate. He then told her to write to the CO of my Regiment in France, and send my birth certificate claiming me out of the service. Now then, one day in

March while we were in the line the OC's orderly came along calling my name. He said "the OC wants you in his dugout at once". I thought, "Oh hell what have I done now?" I had not done anything. My thoughts went back to the "Sighting of those machine guns" a while ago. It can't be that. Anyway I arrived, stood smartly to attention and saluted. He looked at me and said, "Name etc, you come from Chipping Campden?" When I said yes he barked, "How old are you?" I said "Nineteen sir". Then he repeated it and I said once again "I am nineteen Sir", then he pointed to my birth certificate on the table, and I said I still wanted to soldier on. Then he said "your mother claims you out, as being underage". I was then sixteen. In the end he said, "You will go back out of here today and get on the train leaving the railhead at "Noeux- Les- Mines" this evening. So I went back, collected my gear and said cheerio to my friends and collected my official papers from the CO office dug out, and cleared off back to Le Havre.

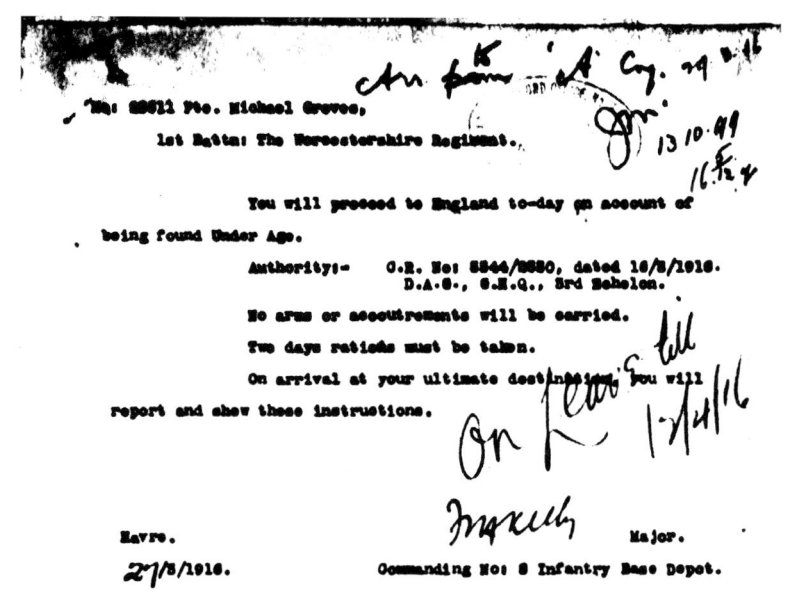

Discharge document being underage

Campden Railway Station

Chapter Four
Return Home

After a day at the Docks, I was put on a cross-channel steamer for England. I still had all my gear, and was weighed down with it. We left Le Havre at four thirty in the afternoon of March 26 1916, and ran full tilt into the blizzard which was raging soon after we sailed, and we finally arrived at Southampton at three thirty next afternoon. There were a lot of troops on board, also two German planes lashed on deck. All hatches were battened down, none could go above and the stench from sickness and foul air was ghastly. This was normally an eight hour trip. It took us twenty three hours. We could not get in past the Needles. My goodness it was rough. A lot of the time I anchored myself to a bench. It was almost impossible to stand and walk about. Also the deck was in a fine mess. However, we finally landed, and I got on a train, arriving at Campden station very late. The telegraph poles and wires were down all along the line.

On the way home I got stuck in the deep snow up to my middle just along from the "Coneygree" gate, then I saw a movement over the wall, by Walker's gate. He had seen me and called out, "Get back out of there and come over here, there's no snow this side of the wall". It was the Gas Man from the Gas House. I went the other side

Grammar School boys clearing snow c1916

of the wall and was walking on dead leaves. The snow had drifted and filled the road six feet deep along the level there. I soon knocked my door to wake someone up to let me in. Next day I went on to Norton Barracks, Worcester, where I was discharged from the service. This early service entitled me to the 1914-1915 medal.

There was no work at the time so I went with Tom Keeley to Birmingham and got a job on munitions at Bordesley Green somewhere. Unfortunately it was not very long before they had a clear out of all young fellows not exempt from service, so I had to leave. I tried all factories and finally got a job at Ward End. This meant new lodgings as well. I got in with some nice folks and there was one other lodger, an older man. The householder was a signalman. My work was as mate to a tool setter. He was a big man and a very good man to be with. The job was looking after the tools in the capstan lathes, tempering and setting, grinding and fitting the cutting tools. We worked a fortnight, days and nights alternately. This job I really enjoyed. I learnt a lot and it was interesting as well. Of course as usual it was too good to last. Once again there was a clear out and I had to go. My mate tried hard to have me kept on but it was not good. I was told I would be wanted over the other side now. Naturally I was upset and cursed him, and said I had already been out there, which was more than he was ever likely to do. But it was not good. I was beginning to feel that fate, or ill luck, was my future companion. In later years this seemed to be very much the case for, although I fought every inch of the way throughout my career I never really got anywhere.

I tried to settle down at home but it was very difficult in several ways and I knew that I should in the end have to move on. However I worked for a time with Teddy Horwood, a silversmith, jeweller and enameller at the Guild. His shop was at the back, the ground floor where Pyments office is. The first part next to the basement was an open space. My first job was to make twenty four MOB School Badges in silver and set with moonstones. These were for a girls school. Then, soon after this, he closed his shop and moved all his gear, and went away to Bognor. So I was out again. I next worked with Joe Warmington for a few weeks. His shop was at the street side of the Guild opposite Horwood. (Now used as part of Pyments office) here we upholstered a suite of furniture. This was quite a nice useful job and it gave me a working knowledge of that kind of work. This job was for a farmhouse on the top road towards Moreton-in-Marsh. The farm was in a dip in the ground. The second gate I think, on the right hand side. Joe sent me up to the house, to tell them the work was finished for them to collect.

About this time, Arthur Pyment had a motorbike, we altered the shape of the petrol tank, also cut the shape of the frame to suit. What a job, it had to be brazed together which was hard to do, however, after several attempts we managed to get it together, all very exciting, but nothing in my pocket. Eventually it seemed all right, so we went to try the machine. You had to push it to start the engine. Joe had the controls and handlebars, we pushed it and the engine came to life but Joe was not quick enough and failed to mount the bike and broke his leg.

Next I went to the shop above, George Hart, silversmith. I was there quite a time and got on famously. I liked old George and he was quite interesting. Again I learnt quite a lot there. It was good to shape things out of flat sheet and draw silver to different thicknesses and shapes of wire. Then fit things and solder on the decorative wires etc.

Quite naturally of course it was very lonely for me as I was the only young chap there and it was all so quiet, apart from the sound of our hammers.

Chapter Five
Return to the Armed Forces

In the end I felt I had to move, and the only thing left was for me to join the Services again. So in the end I put my age on a bit and on the 4th May 1917 I joined "The Royal Marine Artillery" at Bristol. This I could only get in by signing on for twelve years. I was told I could get free discharge at the end of the war, as they would be over strength. They guaranteed this. So off I went to Portsmouth to their depot at Eastney Barracks. My age recorded on my register sheet details, were 17 years, 11 months and 21 days. It was also recorded that I was under age from the 4th May to 12th May. My trade was recorded as a silversmith.

Mike Grove on right aged 17 with mates in Royal Marine Artillery 1917

We were formed into a squad of sixty for training and my squad number was sixty. I am given a regimental no. 15616 and then followed training which was to the limit of severity. As I had done military training before I was well equipped to cope with it, but the power, precision and extent of it was tremendous. Nothing in the world was better than us, and the work in the gym was really something. I reckon we were ready to jump out of our skins and I went all through the training as a candidate for promotion. I never did get anywhere, but of course I was young and promotion was very slow in this Service. After passing out on the parade ground we were put into trained men's quarters, which was better for us, for discipline in the recruit's room was fearful. Beds lined up, clothing and equipment laid out in a special manner. All brass polished buckles and tag ends. The floor scrubbed white. Table gear exactly right and quarters examined and inspected every morning by the officer of the day and his followers.

During this training we had swimming in the afternoons and had to pass out doing six lengths of the bath wearing a "duck suit". The suit I had to wear for this was miles too big and I was dragging tons of water in this big thing as I ploughed along. I just made it. I remember I was too loaded to get out at the end. There seemed gallons of water running out as I eventually got on top. Phew! What a test. That ended the swimming.

We all had to go to school to get our third class education. Anyone who failed this was put out of the regiment. Actually I sat for my second class certificate, the very first day we were taken to school. The schoolmaster sent me in to sit, as there was a 2nd class exam just started. You see I had told him I had been to a grammar school when he took particulars of us. I completed the exam and was soon out and obviously I knew I had passed. Then it went up in orders and it was entered on my sheet. So now I had an hour to myself in the afternoons while the others were at school. But I still had to sit for my "Third," it was routine they said, but it did not take long. I was away in twenty minutes, I remember this well.

Next we went for Sea Service Training. During this I learnt all about knots and lashings, all forms of rope work and steel rope as well, fixing, splicing etc. We also had land service at the "Fort," where we did Bridge Building and Derricks and Shears, also moving guns with ropes. In sea service battery we learnt all about gunnery up to the fifteen inch guns in turrets. If anyone did not pay attention they were given a hundred pound six inch shell to nurse, and that took a bit of holding for a time. We had in the end a test of gun laying. Two groups of five shots, best group and time to the winner. There was a one inch aiming barrel screwed into the breech of a six inch gun. This was done to save expense (better than shooting six inch shells). The gun was set up to simulate a battle ship rolling and pitching at sea, and you had to spin the elevating wheel to keep on target. Now I assure you this is hard work. You had to fire the gun as and when you were ready. I was good at any form of shooting and anyway I took first prize with the best two groups in the quickest time too. Of course it made me "stick my chest out" when the Senior Officer said his piece. He said "its such men as you, who are the future gunners of the service". Those were his actual words. Naturally we went on the range for rifle firing as well. It was a full course, one hundred to one thousand yards range, single shots and groups. This I came through with "flying colours". Still, as boys at home we were always shooting with an air gun. I used to stand a bit of candle on the ledge of the garden door, and light it and from perhaps ten to fifteen yards away, shoot the flame out. So you see I was well used to accurate shooting. As well as all the rounds I had fired in the Worcester Regiment during my previous service in France. There, in the line, I often at night fired at the flashes of the Gerry machine guns when they opened up. Hoping that I might by luck hit someone.

Now that our training is complete I volunteered for land service. Now the R.M.A had twelve fifteen-inch Howitzers. One in England for training and the rest in France. There were only these twelve made. We trained on this one for a few days and then went to camp with it, actually mounting and going through the motions of firing, then dismounting. This took on an average eight hours to dismount if things went well. Each gun had six sixty-horsepower tractors (similar to a steam roller for style) but with small front wheels instead of a roller. We had to dig a pit twenty one feet square about three feet deep, and level it off. Then fit sixteen bed plates, seven girders on top and fix girder transomes on top all bolted together. Then the "cradle" and gun fitted on that. There was a hoist and bay for the shell, which weighed on average, fourteen hundred pounds, and the charge which was in a circular case went into the Breech after the shell was rammed home. The charge weighed fifty six pounds. A detonator was inserted into a place in the breech blocks, and the gun was fired by electric current, using a plunger box which was fifteen to twenty feet behind the gun. All the crew had to stand behind, facing and relaxed, as the shock of discharge was considerable.

Chapter Six
Return to France for the second time

Now the time has come for us to be sent overseas. Up until now our uniform has been blue but now we are fitted out in khaki and given seven days draft leave and then over we go. We sail from Dover to Calais on 31st May 1918. I am sent with others to gun number twelve. They were mounting in a new position near a farm, and at midday meal most of the men went into a barn, and while inside, a German eight inch shell dropped straight in there and killed and wounded nineteen men. There were two gun crews of twelve men so nearly all of them were put out of action. We arrived just in time, so helped to mount the gun. We had our own transport and drivers etc. as well as the two crews. Our rations came though naval sources and there was a doctor for the total guns.

As the range of our gun was only eleven thousand yards, we were always close up near the sixty pounders. Still we were able to make ourselves reasonably comfortable, in dugouts and made paths to the gun area. Also we were able to keep clean. No more vermin (lice). One of the last positions we were in, near the end of the war was just behind Kemmel Hill, about two kilometres away. This was a hill with a flat top. About this time a nine-two Naval gun, mounted on a railway truck with two or three other box wagons attached for ammunition and crew use. This set up would be pushed up a railway line, to a given point. Then the engine went away, later to return and take them away after they had done their "shoot". This was about a kilometre on our left and we could see all that went on. (The ground here is quite flat).

Anyway during this, time they had fired three rounds and then they had a "premature". The shell burst in the barrel. This was terrible. It wiped out most of the crew. What with shock and metal from the explosion it was terrible. I beg your forgiveness if this has bored you who may read it but I felt I just had to describe our guns and also the nine-two naval. You see in the weekly booklet of the "Great War" published during or just after the war one picture print I saw showed our fifteen inch gun, with a caption "Heavy Artillery manned by Australian Gunners". This of course was altogether wrong, as the Royal Marines had the only guns of this type.

I remember the morning of the final attack, September 17th or 27th 1918, which finished off the enemy. About half past two to three am. All hell was let loose. Thousands of guns firing, flashes from them lit up all around. There was quite a breeze blowing towards Gerry and fine rain all the time. Of course when the boys went forward guns had to go as well. Once that happened we were soon out of range. No more shooting for us. By the time we had dismounted the gun they were a good way ahead.

By the way signalmen who could be spared had to go, to carry and lay new lines, following the advance. One chap went from our lot. Then as we moved forward we saw him sitting on the foothills of Hill Sixty. He had some food in his hand but was quite dead. No visible damage but there was a very small shell hole close to him, quite fresh. So we thought shock must have done it. We went on and stayed on the roadside near a cross roads for our food. Then a Red Cross train (this means a complete outfit with all their road transport) pulled up on the grass verge, from another direction at the cross roads, when all of a sudden the whole outfit went up. The grass verge must have been mined. One never forgets wholesale carnage. Time makes it vague, that's all.

We now continued through Ypres (when I first went through here with the Worcesters, the beautiful Cloth Hall had not been damaged) but now it, like most other places was in ruins, battered to pieces. We went through what is now the "Menin Gate" along the Menin Road, and through Paschendalle

[*Passchendaele*], here was an area where it was just one mass of shell holes, and water, you could not step between holes full of filth. Of course some of the bitterest fighting took place here.

Finally we arrived at "Coutrai" [*Kortrijk*]. That was the furthest we went, later we worked our way back and stopped for Christmas at a village called "Widnes", we all clubbed together and bought a pig to roast for Christmas dinner. (One of our fellows was a butcher). I'm afraid no one had any of it. Everyone got boozed up on various French wines. The pig was roasted to a cinder. No one seemed to care anyway and I'm afraid I was as bad as the rest. Soon after this, we moved on, and finally arrived at a tiny fishing village right on the Sea front. We were billeted in an old "Casino". It was quite empty but dry.

Ypres - present day photo!

Menin Gate - present day photo!

Chapter Seven
End of World War 1

I was given leave to U.K. from 17th January 1919 to 6th February 1919, It was during the time of a very bad flu epidemic, people were dying everywhere. One of the Keyte's from Mickleton Hills went while I was home. I too failed with it when I returned to France, and I don't remember a thing for a complete week, but was soon all right.

We had to hang on here for a good time, until we were allowed to hand in the gun etc. While we were there, some of us had a two day trip to Ostend and Zeebrugge, to see where the ships had been sunk to close the harbours for Gerry. We also called at Bruges. This I thought was a nice town, and the Cathedral was beautiful. They had a carillon of forty eight bells there and they played some nice tunes on them.

Finally we managed to get away. I think this was in May 1919. As soon as we reached our Depot at Portsmouth we were given seven days leave, then all time serving men were fitted out in blue, and sent to various ships until such time as our discharge came through. I with one or two others went to join HMS Revenge.

HMS Revenge

She was stood off Southend. We were taken out in the ships pinnace, the ship was rolling a good deal and as the pinnace steamed slowly past one had to jump for the rope ladder, now, this was not funny at all. We were all in full marching order, which in itself was enough. One second you were hanging on, about two yards out, then, as she rolled you slammed against the ships side. I was thankful to be dragged on board when I reached deck level, and never want that experience again. This ship was one of the "First Battle Squadron", we were the flagship with Vice Admiral Sir Sidney Fremantle on board. The names of the ships in the Squadron were Revenge, Ramilles, Resolution, Royal Oak, Royal Sovereign and Queen Elizabeth. All armed with four two-gun turrets of fifteen inch guns. They all had what we called "concrete blisters", cast on their sides, at, and below the water line, as a protection against torpedoes and mines. This made the ships roll a great deal in even a moderate swell.

By the way on the funnels of our tractors in France were painted the names of a Naval Squadron, Invincible, Indefatigable, Indomitable, unfortunately I forget the rest. There were six.

While I was on the Revenge we called at all the seaside places on the East Coast up to North Scotland. Showing off the ships to the people. We went up the river and under the Forth Bridge, paid a visit to Edinburgh and played inter ship football on Dunfermline's ground. Here I left to return to Portsmouth where I was discharged. This was at the end of 1919.

Extract from Research Records:

On discharge he was recommended for the Royal Fleet Reserve (RFR). No indication of joining the RFR is noted. Ed

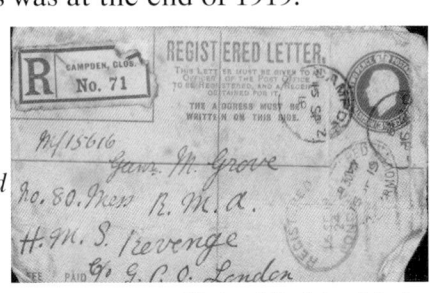

Photo of Registered Letter

Chapter Eight
Civilian Street once more
work very scarce

I found civilian life very dull. There seemed to be no work at all, and of course one had to get about and pick up what one could. Perhaps a bit of threshing. There were no combines then. I once dug a patch of potatoes at the Research Station. It was the biggest crop I have ever seen. The potatoes covered the ground. I did not have to pick them up though. Oh, I went into South Wales for a time. But I could not afford to live there. Everything was so expensive. The miners were getting about three times the money we could earn. They all grumbled but they were well off to what we were. I'd had enough so I cleared off home.

Now I spent five pounds on special typed application for a job on tea, sugar and rubber plantations, but all replies were negative. They all said they were now back to full strength. No vacancies.

While at home I joined the local branch of the Worcester Territorials. My friends were in it. We went to camp in Wales near Conway. That was not very special either. It poured with rain and the tents were mostly waterlogged although we dug trenches round. The camp should have been pitched on higher ground. We were flat and low. However I made a visit to Conway Castle. By the way being in this lot you were another number. Before they were Regimental numbers now this was an Army number 5244612. I wonder if anyone else had three different numbers?

I feel I must say a few things about our local characters and goodness they are numerous. I suppose all country villages especially, had their share. Some of these were very witty. A few of these types were always to be found around the market. This was a monthly affair. The square in Campden was used to pen the sheep. These pens were made of wooden hurdles, tied together to form a square. On some occasions these pens took up a lot of the spare time, especially when the sheep were brought in off the hills where they had fed on kale. Their wool was brownish from being on the ground but they looked fat and well. The pigs, calves and cattle were penned in the sale yard at the back of the Noel Arms. I had the job to put this new sale area together. It was the old sale yard from Worcester which the local people had purchased. It was quite a game sorting it out and adapting it to suit our layout here. This work was carried out in the winter time. We did it really to find work for the men, as work was very scarce then. My word it took some sticking what with rain and then frost on the ironwork and mud and filth most of the time. You know when it was very frosty it meant a rag or bag in one's hand, when dealing with this ironwork, otherwise it might take the skin off your hand.

In recent years this was all cleared away as these markets were finished with. Animals were then transported to Stratford etc. to the bigger permanent sales yards. All are carried in transporter motor-wagons now, (No more driving them by road) for motor traffic was fast developing and now at this time traffic here is very busy. Some of those local characters were always at the sales. They used to drive animals in batches from the market to their new destination at some farm or other, and mostly to the railway, where they were loaded into railway trucks for despatch to Birmingham.

These "drovers" hung about all day for a shilling or so, and of course for cider or beer in the pubs.

At the time I am writing about, Tiger Smith and Lawrence Ladbrook (he was quite a young chap then) used mostly to make up these hurdle pens on market day. Then they had to dismantle and cart them back to their store at the back of the Noel, and clean up the Square after. The auctioneers were "Taylor and Fletcher" from Stow. Later on there was the wool to deal with. It was packed in very large sacks and finally sent off by rail. The sheep being sheared during late May or early June.

One of the noted "drovers" was Charles Seitz (Sykes). He was a very tall dark man. I would say there was a bit of Indian in his make up. Actually as I understand it he was born in India. He lived in Leasebourne in the house now "The Convent". He had a darkie Nanny and later was studying to become a doctor, but his brain let him down so he could not continue to study, and in the end lived alone in a cottage in Back Ends, and spent the rest of his time going to market as a "drover".

Laurence Ladbrook previously mentioned, also did the job of Town Crier, but that, like lots of old customs, died out. I think the bell and cocked hat is still in his possession.

Another outstanding character was Charles 'Slap', Blakeman. A sort of horse breaker, dealer, full of rough jokes. Always in debt and nearly always drunk. He with old Ted (Edwin Ladbrook, Lawrence's father) and Joe Fairweather, (Wetlegs as he was called) were a right lot. I imagine their wives had a very poor time. Short of cash and much to put up with.

Quite often there were workmen who suddenly went on the drink for two or three days. The pubs were open almost all day at that time. I suppose these chaps got drunk and lay about until they sobered up a bit, then went on again, and just as suddenly, they would appear back at work as though nothing had happened. Where they found the money from goodness knows. They must have kept their wives very short of cash. I know the cider and beer was very cheap at that time. I heard of a man going out and getting quite "tiddly" and buying some tobacco and still having change out of a shilling! I know a farm hand whose week's pay was fourteen shillings a week at the beginning of the first war 1914. Things were cheap. Even so, it was a tight existence. Children did not have pocket money like they do today. A half penny was about the lot, once a week.

It might be interesting to list the pubs in Campden. They may not have all been open at one time. Anyway past and present, there they are. The "Royal Oak", "Volunteer", "Rose and Crown", "The Plough", "Red Lion", "Green Dragon", "Noel Arms", the "Live and Let Live", "The Swan", "The Lygon Arms", "The George and Dragon", "The Eight Bells", "The Barley Mow", "The Kettle" this was an outdoor licence. I understand "Peyton House" was also a pub. It may have been especially for the workers at that place making twine. There are still the cottages called Twine Cottages at the back of Peyton House. By the way I converted the building (which was the place of twine making), into a dwelling, several years ago. This Peyton House is next to the Baptist Chapel, and took in the property on the opposite side of the wide entry.

After all when one thinks, that at that time, beer, cider and home made wine were about the only drink apart from water. Tea was very costly and only for the rich, being from China, and only a very small import. Later, tea was also cultivated in India and Ceylon, becoming more plentiful and affordable, which soon changed the mode of drinking.

The demand for alcohol drink must have been great at one time, when one thinks of the Silk Mill, later to become the Guild of Handicrafts, the railway, and with its tunnel to be built, as well as all the other jobs going on. Yes it must have been a thriving thing then.

There were a good many odd characters about in these days. Some to be made fun of, and some very witty, who had an answer for anything. You think about these various people and realise that they made the place, made life more tolerable, created fun for many. Look at this list of names, "Forty Merriman", "Ninety Griffin", "Warrier Smith", "Canadian Jack Coldicott", "Fudger Yates", "Jigger James", "Tiger Smith", "Flago Smith", "Nezzie Plested" "Pawty Skey", "Joey (Wetlegs) Fairweather", "Charlie Slap Blakeman", "Ben the Busman

Benfield", " "Bob Minchin" deaf and dumb mute, "Steve Hancock", "Charlie Sykes", "Bob Haines", "Jim Sharpe," "Blacksmith Haydon". Oh what a splendid sample these were. There are lots more who were prominent in their day, Polly Wain, Sarah Brotheridge. These two especially. Then we had fine workmen with their little trader's shops. Charlie Withers, Blacksmith, one of the best, Tom Barnes also a Blacksmith. Tom Ellison "Saddler", Harry Ellis, basket maker with Dennis Hathaway and Fred in the basket shop. (That was good). J.W. Pyment at the Guild, He was Town Bandmaster for years. We also had George Hart a wonderful silversmith – my good friend years ago. Alec Miller, fine sculptor. These were operating at the Guild. There are many more I could mention. All excellent men, all going together to make Campden a great place, although we youngsters did not think about it in that way then. Charlie Withers the Blacksmith made lots of tools for me, and sharpened and tempered and drew out, these, as I required. He was very neat and could make most things such as window frames etc. I think I learnt quite a bit by watching him at work for I used to spend a good bit of time in his shop, when I was a lad.

   In those days lighting was by oil lamps, or candles. The street lamps were lit by gas, but how very poor they were, just a flame then, gas mantles came later, and I can assure you that it was no fun getting about in winter time, what with mud and bad light. Not like today (clean roads and paths). One mostly crouched by the fire until sent to bed, out of the way. Still, everyone went to bed early then, for those who had work, were up early, as they had to walk to work wherever it was.

New council houses in Aston Road, being built for returning servicemen

Chapter Nine
Chance of work improving

Now work is looking up. Building is going on, so I am able to get at it. I worked on the County Council houses, Aston Road, Campden. There were also two blocks built in Station Road, and four blocks of two at Broad Campden. At that time most of the materials were carted in horse drawn vehicles. Anyway 1921 was a good year for work, also it was the hottest and driest for many years. I did work at Saintbury, Old School House and at the vicarage there.

Then work faded out again, unemployment everywhere. So in 1922 I obtained a job as steward on the Red Star Liner Lapland. That line operated from Antwerp to New York, calling at Southampton and Cherbourg. Other ships of this company were Zeeland, Groonland and Finland. I did two trips on this ship but it was not good to me. We started at three thirty am washing floors, cleaning and laying tables, and it was after eleven pm before we were finished. I packed the job in after these two runs. It did not suit me being below decks all the time, and I suppose I was quite a bit love-sick as well.

Anyway work was beginning to improve again in the building line, and I was soon going full time. We used to work a fifty hour week, often longer. We did two houses in Station Road, Campden, and then two more at Willersey, and an alteration at Pool Farm. I think we worked from about 7.30 am till 6.00 pm, at one time 6.30 pm. We used to cycle. Sometimes I walked with the old hands. You had to be there for start time and did not get away till knock off. No travelling in firm's time then. I used to have to cycle into Broadway to get the wage money from the bank. The employer then was a John Wayne from Gretton. Not a bad fellow at all, but like the rest of us he had no money. He had to get a cheque off the owners each week, at any rate he was fair.

In the end the work with him was finished. So it was time to get another job. I began work with J.W. Pyment and Sons early in 1924 where we had a splendid run of work, starting with Mr Dewey's house, then several houses in Station Road. I was now right on top form with top rate of pay. (This was poor enough pay) in these times. Real sweated labour. So you can tell, we only lived week to week, no savings.

Now I was beginning to make my presence felt, by the quantity and quality of my work. I was given charge of jobs now, and used to see them through from start to finish. Also I did a good deal of stone working. Some of it in spare time and weekends, mullion windows, kneelers and apex stones, copings and moulded work. I did a big balustrade which is now in the garden at Norman Chapel.

Carved ballustrade Norman Chapel

Photo taken by kind permission of the owner

All of this stone working was, with stone as quarried, no saws then. There were grave stones and memorials of all kinds, and I worked a lot with Alec Miller, he was a famous sculpter. One Easter time, I worked on a Portland Stone head for him, all Friday, Saturday and Easter Monday until four pm. Several times I had told him there was a flaw in the stone, but he said, "oh carry on it may be all right", but I knew it was no good. In the end, after all that work, I left it in disgust. All that work for nothing, as well as the holiday I had missed, still that was a hazard one has to face. However he brought me out, encouraged me to go on, with a hint here and there, until I could turn out quite intricate jobs.

I once worked a fortnight on a life size of a squatting figure which we called the "Sphinx". It was of a girl kneeling, with her face supported on her elbows and hands. Alec kept urging me to go on, and said, "get the feel of the line of ribs, and the general flow of the body".

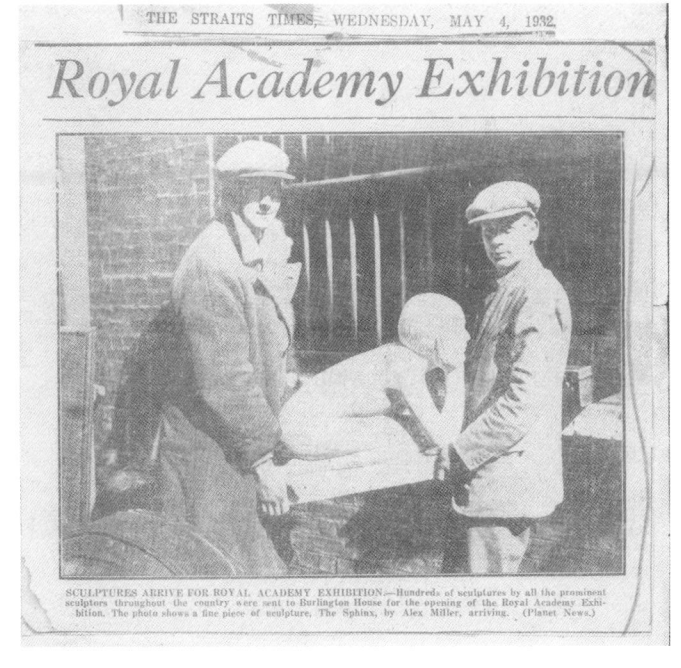

"Sphinx" being carried into Royal Acadamy Exhibition by Michael Grove and Fred Coldicott 1932

This was done in Caen Stone (French). Alec put a little time on the eyes and toes, I did all the rest. We took this figure to Burlington House London, where it was accepted into the Academy. Fred Coldicott, Pyment's lorry driver, and myself carried it in. There is a newspaper picture of us taking it in.

I did a good bit of letter cutting too on all the memorials I handled. Also about this time I carved out of big blocks of stone from Guiting the tops of the pinnacles on the tower. It ought to have been harder stone but I had to use what they provided.

I took a sixteen-foot-high crucifix carved by Alec to Formby Churchyard near to Southport also I did a headstone in Hopton Wood for him, it had a sunken panel with moulded edges and carved leaves. I took this and fixed it in St Mary's Churchyard Wimbledon. I also carved an "Obelisk" in Mansfield Stone for Lapworth churchyard, that was in 1933.

St Mary's Churchard, Wimbledon
Left: Obelisk in Lapworth Churchyard

I also fixed on the sloping window-sill inside a church at Nottingham or was it Northampton? A beautiful figure carved and painted by Alec Miller. I had to cut a recess in the sill to set it in level. Fred Coldicott was our lorry driver and so was with me on all these occasions.

I married my dear wife at Whitsun, 1925. This became the most precious part of my life but I shall not write about it as it is a personal thing. Except to say that we have two fine sons.

Michael and his wife Edith (nee Benfield) at the time of their marriage 1925

Now back to work. My firm had priced a big job at Minchinhampton only because I had said I would do it if it came along. This was early in 1927. The result was that the job was ours. All Pyment had to do was sign the documents. I was working at Saintbury at the time. Harold came down in his car and told me about it, and I said "I will do it". So he took me back to the office where we talked it over. I said "yes", otherwise they would turn it down.

45

It was a large house with cottage and garage, long drive and entrance gates, with shaped stone wall and pillars. Actually I was there thirteen months. We lodged in a cottage close to the work. My wife and son Tony. I still have a letter of thanks etc, from the owner, Mr Sidney Wales.

Time goes on, and there were quite a few jobs we did (but only on condition I was on the job). I do not like to think I am bragging but it was so. I always tried to give my best in the quickest way. In those times building was heavy work. Concrete was all mixed by hand. The aggregate was stone, broken by hand hammers, so was rough and it was hard to handle, being coarse, it was hard work to get a fatty surface and to level it. There were no concrete mixers about. They came later, as did the new type of plastic. What a blessing they were. They took a lot of hard work away from jobs.

My next big job was at Westington Mill, Campden, difficult but interesting. Here, I copied a canopy over the entrance to "Poppits Alley", and set it up over the front door. I worked at this in my spare time.

Stone canopy, Poppet's Alley

Stone canopy, Westington Mill

Photo taken by kind permission of the owner

I had to do a lot of work "spare time" to find money to pay doctor's bills. Wages were not much in those days, about one shilling and four pence per hour for trades and ninepence for labour, and of course unless there was a job under cover, you lost all wet time. Also although I was in charge of work, I never had any benefits, I only had what I worked for. I controlled the big house in Sheep Street for Ralph Heaton and even corrected the Architect's mistakes. He showed a beam, carrying a gutter over the main landing at four foot nine from the floor. I found this out when I was measuring up the timber required for the roof etc. This job involved taking down two or three cottages to prepare the site.

I also handled the first two houses in the "Clay Garden" site, now called "Grevel Lane".

TELEGRAMS:	**J. W. PYMENT & SONS,**	STATION:
PYMENT, CAMPDEN.	BUILDERS, JOINERS, CABINET-MAKERS,	CAMPDEN, G.W.RLY.
TELEPHONE:	AND ECCLESIASTICAL WOODWORKERS,	PARTNERS:
CAMPDEN 233.	**CAMPDEN,**	H. G. PYMENT, A. S. PYMENT.
	GLOS.	

TO WHOM IT MAY CONCERN.

    The Bearer of this note, Mr. M.P. Grove, has been employed by us for the past 16 years, for the last 13 years in the capacity of General Foreman.

    We have always found him strictly honest, sober and thoroughly reliable in the management of jobs and men, and we can, with every assurance, recommend him for any position in the supervision of jobs or the management of men.

    His only reason for leaving us, is with a view to joining the Royal Engineers, for the period of the War, and we shall be quite willing to place him in his old position, on his return.

                   FOR & ON BEHALF OF
                    J. W. PYMENT & SONS.

                                PARTNER.

Testimonial letter from J W Pyment & Sons 1940

Chapter Ten
Beginning of World War 2
Back to France for the third time, and finally Dunkirk

We are now beginning to hear murmurs of war. Hitler was bent on grabbing more land and everyone thinks it is a bluff. But not so. Gerry had amassed tremendous quantities of all requirements, including tanks by the thousand. This threat finally came about in September 1939. Territorials were called up and work was rapidly closing down. I naturally thought that the state would take control of everything. (Labour and food under strict control). But as in the first war, Black Market was rampant and many men got out of everything.

The state was calling for volunteers to work on the defences in Belgium. I thought, perhaps, it was a temporary job. Anyway, with brother Bob, we joined January 1st 1940. We were sent to Clacton where we were all trade tested by senior officers of the Engineers. I went before a Major and showed him the testimonial from J W Pyment which I took with me.

I also told him of my previous Services as well as discussed construction. He then put everything down on his sheet, in red ink and told me that as soon as we were formed up into a working company I would automatically be made "Section Sergeant". I had nothing to worry about. No need for any other test or questions - those were his exact words.

It was wicked weather this winter. A lot of snow and sharp frosts and winds. Anyway we were counted off into the required number for a company, and then sent off to Margate, which was our depot for training before going abroad. We paraded next day, or whenever it was. I am not quite sure of this date, to be told all the list of promotions and officers. I listened to it all, but as usual with the typical "Grove's" luck my name was not mentioned. I felt very disappointed as I had been assured that I was to be a sergeant. We did some drills, marching on the sands, that was the only place as deep snow was everywhere. I had to laugh once or twice while we were out at drill. Often we were given ridiculous orders and at times I called out "there's no such order in the British Army". The NCO in charge said "Come out here and have a go". I quickly told him he was the one with the stripes. "Try again" I said. I had trained as a candidate for promotion, in the finest regiments in the world. It was bad, very bad, training in that snow and cold. Of course we all had our inoculations etc. while we were there. One of these was tough. Fairly bowled the chaps out, later at night.

One day I was called to go to the CO's office, and when I arrived he told me I had not had a trade test. I was flabbergasted, and let my annoyance be noticed. I said a naughty word or two, begging his pardon. Told him what had happened at Clacton "Trade Test". I showed him Pyments letter as well. He said "you send that back home for safe keeping". He was sorry but nothing could be done now as all the promotions had been made and were official. Not his doing at all. He also said he would do what was possible when we were over the other side. Of course I knew I would not get anywhere, unless an NCO was put out of action.

After a couple of weeks or thereabouts, we got sent over to France complete with working kit and transport. The transport Section goes off in front, as advance party. They have to find accommodation for the Company, on arrival. What a joint it was too. We finally arrived at the nearest railhead. A place called "Orchies". Oh what a state some of the chaps were in. They'd had their boots off in the train and as their feet had swollen had a job to get their boots on again. We all had our kit to carry and two blankets each, and a good two miles to march up the cobbled road. (I carried Bob's stuff, or some of it) we arrived at a small village called "Nomain", and were put in farm buildings. They were very poor and the conditions were worse. Its very flat country just there and the water in the well was only about six foot down, the ditches were level, full of stagnant water when it thawed a bit, it was a very unhealthy place. later when I did go into Orchies, you could see that the house refuse, water, sewerage material was piped out under the pavement and into the gutters. Still I knew from years before that these people were a dirty, scruffy lot.

Soon after this I was made a lance-corporal. By the way I was given my army number. They asked previous servicemen for their number. I said I had three lots and gave them 23611 Worcesters, 15616 Royal Marines and 5244612 army number. This was the one I was officially given now. So my address here was 5244612 L/Cpl. M.P. Grove, No.4 Section, 660 General Construction Co. B.E.F. France. This was early February 1940.

We discovered our job was to continue the defences along the Belgian frontier. The French Maginot line defence ended at the junction with the Belgian /French frontier, so that there was really nothing to deter the Germans if and when he came through Belgium. It was all so stupid. Still I suppose they must have known that what we were doing would hardly do anything to stop him. I used to say to the men I was with "look at the open area in front of us. There, only a concrete Pill-Box about every three hundred yards apart. Do you think Gerry will come one at a time to get knocked off". Besides the arms which were proposed for these places would scarcely stop anything and I said he will come in hundreds when he does attack and with Lord knows how many aircraft to soften it up. We have not got a cat in hell's chance of stopping him.

I had a bright Sgt. in charge of my section. He was a coal heaver in civil life. Another was a labourer. Anyway my Sgt. came out with us to the job we were on, and left ME to handle and do all the work and went off rabbiting or whatever. He used to get back just before it was time for the transport to take us back to our billets. As far as trade work was concerned there were those of these Sgt's. not worth a light. They relied on their tradesmen to get the work done, but were slick with their tongues otherwise. It was typical of the service "All the round pegs were in the square holes", and oh dear me when the thaw came it was just sheer nasty thick yellow mud. Oh God, what a mess to live and work in. It was enough to kill anyone. That and the bad water and terrible food.

I came off guard one morning and the sergeant got me to go off straight away to the job. I felt awful too, for I could now hardly move as I had suddenly developed prolapsed haemorrhoids (piles). I could not sit, only lean forward over a table. I had to go sick and was finally sent back to Two GCS. Then back by ambulance to the next place where, after they gave me gas and put these things back, I was put on a Red Cross train, and went back to a tented hospital. The only decent treatment I ever had was on this train. WVS ladies or whoever they were gave us comforts and kind words which I never forgot. Military hospital people treated us very badly indeed. I have no good word at all for them. In time I had my operation (no attention after it at all) and as soon as one could crawl about there was work for you to do.

I was glad to get away from there and more so to get back to my own Unit. I at least had some friends there. Also I knew our CO. Tom Cross looked on me a bit with favour. He knew I knew what I was doing at work. I even showed another Section Sgt. how to set about and do the steel-loop hole in his pill box. Actually he was a real "Basket" an old sweat with a bayonet scar all down his face. But when I had shown him and told him to do exactly as I said, he found it was right, I was it to him. He thanked me plenty for it, as he had no idea at all.

Now real trouble is brewing. Gerry is beginning to come our way. My section had to go forward to Tournai to do an urgent road job. We were billeted in a Casino in the middle of the street. Wide open to anything.

This one morning, I spotted in the distance like a swarm of

flies 47 Gerry planes coming our way. Phew, I thought, this is our lot. They just passed over us and bombed Tournai. Gave it a real bashing and also set the church on fire. At night, he kept coming over, the burning tower was a good guide for him. Seemed to go into his attacking dive just over our heads then all hell let loose. We were carted back to our Unit soon after this. They were setting up anti-tank guns in the street as we pulled out, so he was not far away.

This of course finished our work. We were moved about more as a fighting unit now sections being put in various places. I noticed several other army units had already moved out. I saw one of our corporals go into a dugout. We never saw him again, he must have run away in the night. Still about this time Gerry was round us in a horscshoe position when lights were fired up at night, you could see we were in a tight hole. Our OC told us so as well.

We had a Bren-gun set up on a tripod, loaded and with a guard on it and this particular day a dose of Gerry planes came over flying low. There was no opposition (in fact I never saw any English planes up) they were like great bats casting shadows on the ground as they went. I said let me have a go, at these. I kept giving bursts of a few rounds at a time, aiming just in front of his nose. After a bit he turned off and headed back home with black smoke pouring out, and I am sure I hit his fuel pipe and maybe the pilot as well. At all events I claimed it as my kill, and later the OC came and said his piece. I felt a bit better after that. But now the CRE is trying to get us away.

We line up under a bank along a side road waiting for transport to come and pick us up, nothing doing, but in time it does come and we get away, but how bad on the road. Thousand of refugees going back and all sorts of transport trying to get along as well. We pass through Armentières, which has just been bombed. It smelt of explosives and was all on fire. (I saw the same thing here in the first war). However we get

53

back as far as Cassel, there we have to dump our packs and heavy stuff, transport as well (this gets fired later). We have to slink off from here when it's dark. With no noise as Gerry is near to this place. We keep on marching until finally we arrive at Dunkirk.

We are marched onto the docks quite expecting to see a ship waiting to take us off. What a joke. No ship, no nothing, we have to split up and look out for ourselves. I left brother Bob in between a lot of large barrels and went off with others to look for food and better shelter. The local people were not very helpful I found. It did them no good for we were soon being plastered with bombs. (Before I left the docks). We saw six Hurricanes coming over; we let out a cheer, as we though they were British, but not so. Gerry was flying them and quickly let us know, he shot us up as he swept over. There is with this writing a small snap which I took out of a railway magazine in Nomain. This is a reasonably detailed map in which I saw places I was in or near during the first and second war and it shows our way to Dunkirk.

Now to get back to Dunkirk when the bombing eased off. About six in the evening I think. We came out of our rabbit holes to see what was what, and about the first thing I saw was a sailor standing in the middle of the street. We then saw others. They were so calm and said "all right boys, the Navy is here to save you". Then they told us to go down on to the beach and to get in parties of 50. Then they would pick us up. But we would have to wade out in the boats.

It was getting dark and looking up the beach I saw what looked like two big headlights of some massive Gerry vehicle. I though this must be it. We are to be mown down like corn. There were a lot of men there by this time. It was a false alarm, for these lights were two parachute flares, close together, drifting our way close to the sand. After a bit I saw a group of naval officers on the beach. So I went up to them and gave a smart salute and said "I am ex Naval, what is going on". They then told me that there was a destroyer alongside the "Mole" leaving in a few minutes, if I could get there. This was some distance down on the beach to the "Mole" and I had to climb up the sea wall as well, this was tough and slippery. I suppose about fifteen feet high, and on a slope of course. Anyway I made it and galloped off along the Mole. There was a big area, where a bomb had blown the plank decking away. I just danced over the girder framework and got to the boat, just as she pulled away. I thought, I can't miss this. There was a sailor standing at the rail. He shouted, "jump boy, I'll grab you". It passed through my mind in a flash. "If you miss the jump you will be down in the dock and the ship's screw will do the rest". However I landed safely on deck and we were on our way. I went down into the 'glory hole' (stokers mess) and was soon eating their beautiful fresh bread and butter and cocoa this was a feast to me. The best food I had for a long time. Many thanks to those boys.

I must dwell a while here. Thinking about these last few weeks. What a poor affair it has all been. There were the French, full of "fifth column" and a useless 'Maginot Line' also there was a forest area with a lake at this side. Not fortified, the Germans would never break through here, but this was just what they did. No trouble to them. Blast the trees out and bridge over the water and they were through in force. We seemed to be a poor ill equipped force. Not much armour, fast vehicles or gun power. The only planes we saw in the air were German. They had masses of everything. I did see a French 'Lysander' plane now and then and Gerry came over and promptly shot it down.

Ah, to go back a bit. As we were coming down the road, making our way past 'Armentieres' there was a team of horses, pulling a big French gun along the road and almost holding up all the traffic. I could understand it in the First War but not now.

At this moment, when I think of things, one morning, when we were in the line in the first War, early on. There were eight anchored balloons up behind the line, with spotters or signalmen in the baskets hanging underneath. However, when Gerry came along in his plane he shot down the lot. He put a burst of fire into each gas bag as he went past. There was no time to winch the balloon men down. You could see the crew jump out of their baskets and parachute down.

Now to get back to the destroyer. As we moved away from the jetty, Dunkirk looked a horrible sight. I was glad to get below and out of it.

Chapter Eleven
Back to England

We landed safely at Dover where we were all put into trains. By the way I gave my rifle up to the naval people on the ship. They were collecting all arms; otherwise I had no intention of letting it go.

On the train I noticed we were travelling westwards and wondered what was going to happen to us. However, in time we arrived at Exeter and there we left the train, and marched into the Devonshire Regt. Barracks. There were plenty of people about, staring at us, as though we were prisoners. I say why afterwards. We were put into huts which were quite comfortable, and where we were given soap, towels, and shaving gear, and went to the big wash place. There, one look in the mirror was enough. We were filthy dirty and rough looking with a couple of days beard, but soon felt better after a clean up. Then, after a good feed were soon asleep. Of course, we were a mixed lot, fellows from all sorts of military depts.

We stayed here a few days while sorting out went on. Then the Engineers, my lot, were taken to Tavistock where the whole unit finally collected. We had a forty eight hour leave. So I arranged for my dear wife and son to come back with me. The Sergeant Major tried to be difficult about it. I slept out of course at our digs. Often, I used my previous military service and medal ribbon which I was wearing, as leverage. However, I said and did many things during the next five years which the service gave me cover for. Nothing wrong of course. I once talked to a Brigadier in a hard fashion, but you can be very sure I know what I was at.

Here at Tavistock we were all checked over, the unfit or doubtful were taken out of the unit and sent to bomb disposal. We were made up to strength and finally moved up to North Scotland where we did a good deal of riveting to the River Tay.

Each evening the section sergeants had to report to the O.C. the amount of work done. Well the damn fools. One gave a false report, saying more than he had actually done, another said about the same, or longer as they thought fit. Naturally after a while they were caught out. They must have covered miles of work, as they had reported. Now it had to be put right. My sergeant asked me how much I could do in a day. I quickly gave him the 'gen', but he'd got to drive the rest, all to do the various things to keep me going full speed. I was a working fool then. Finally, I became too careless. In my speed, I slashed open my left wrist with the bill hook I was using. The job was like basket making, lacing in and out of vertical poles with brush wood (like wattle hurdles) only about sixteen feet high in places against the bank, with the soles anchored to stakes in the ground some distance away.

This was supposed to form a tank trap if the Germans ever came! I had my wife up here for a month. This was very good for both of us. Later we moved on to Kinross Airfield for a time, then to Inverness and from there to Elgin where we were in billets in peoples houses, and from there to Lossiemouth. When we were there, one Saturday evening as their planes were coming in to land they were followed by two German planes. They dropped their bombs as they passed over but they were too low. They were just a bit too cheeky. Also whilst we were there I was taken to see a big job at 'Huntley'. This was to build a hutted camp. I was, by this time a L.Sgt. This job was going to make me a WO1, but, luck was not with me, for our unit was suddenly sent to Dyce Aerodrome near Aberdeen and my job was cancelled. Actually, I went sort of advance to the unit. My job was to find and arrange accommodation for our company in peoples' houses. I had fixed up most of the requirements and found a good place where my wife could stay. Then, all of a sudden, the Company was recalled to Aldershot. I knew what this meant. Anyway, I had my wife there until we left.

Chapter Twelve
Drafted Middle East

We were fitted out with tropical kit and finally went to Liverpool in March 1941, where we embarked on the 'Andes'. This was a brand new ship launched in Belfast in 1938. There were still a few stewards on her and, wonder of wonders, four of us were put in a four berth, first class cabin on C deck, port side, with a port hole open to the sea. The cabin had its own bunks, blankets, and also a shower and a toilet. There was also a steward to look after these cabins. I never had it so good. The men were down in the 'holds'. Of course there were thousands of troops on board, but I was lucky indeed. I was never called for any ship duties, only to drill and train my own section. We did quite a bit of PT. Of course, there were a good few ships in the convoy when we finally sailed.

We sailed two-thirds of the way towards America at first. Then the convoy doubled back at an angle before making our first stop anchoring off Freetown, on the north-west coast of Africa (Sierra Leone). Next, we sailed and stopped at Cape Town, South Africa. After a few days, when we went ashore to stretch our legs, we found the people very kind indeed. There were lots of them with their cars by the dock gates to take anyone for a run round the place and give them a 'feed'. You could have anything you like, but it was their custom for you to help to get it yourself. They were very friendly indeed.

We later sailed again, going on up through the Indian Ocean. Of course, our speed was that of the slowest ship in the convoy. One did break down, but we had to keep going, hoping it would catch us up. We heard the warning that there were German submarines about. (By the way this ship had fixed on its stern deck, a six inch BL Mk7 gun which was exactly like one I had trained with in the marines). So I got with the gun crew whenever they did a practice. They did fire a few.

One evening when the German news came on we heard Lord Haw-Haw say "Germany calling, Germany calling, saying our submarines attacked a convoy in the Indian Ocean and sank the Andes and damaged others." We laughed at this, as it was untrue, but it showed what lies the Germans could say.

Well, it was six weeks since we left Liverpool, we passed up the Red Sea and as we were in sight of Suez docks we could see those two magnificent ships the Queen Mary and Queen Elizabeth, what a sight they were. They had travelled on their own, no escort, as they were fast enough to keep out of danger. They were busy off-loading troops and stores etc. Now it was our turn. We left the ship and with all our kit went by train to a camp not far from the Pyramids, to get acclimatised to the conditions. Here it was a dry dusty heat. Of course we were used to the sun by now after our long journey out. (By the way, they held the ceremony of Crossing the Line (Equator) on the ship. Father Neptune did a crude shaving act on a patient who was then tipped backwards into the swimming pool.)

While we were at this camp, I wandered off a bit into a 'sort of sand dunes' and noticed what I took to be mica in among the shale 'sort of muck'. It could have been of no value. While I was looking about, I entered into a sort of fold in the dunes and there facing me was a great big Hyena. Phew, it was about as big a donkey and had quite a mane on its neck. I don't know which of us was most surprised. I thought I had better stand still as I did not have my rifle with me. Anyway, after a few seconds he turned away and loped off. I was very glad. I suppose they are cowards really, but I felt I could trust nothing.

I had my first bottle of beer at this camp, it was quite warm and we had to drink out of the bottle. It upset my tummy so no more like that. Now we move on again. It was a toss up as to whether we stay in the western desert or go to Palestine. Number 59 company stays, and we are put on a train again and go into Palestine. We end up at a camp miles from anywhere.

We stay here for a little while.

Now there is trouble with the Vichy French. These are French troops who have been here mixed with Syrians and other Arabian troops. This little war breaks out and our side push them back pretty fast. They blow the cliff road away in several places as they go back. I was sent with two lorries to Tel Aviv. I had to meet an RE captain who took me with him in his car. He was getting compressors, hose, jack hammers, drills and spades from bits of works and workshops. We went to about eight places. When he took me back to our lorries he asked me if I though I could find those shops etc again. Hell, I thought, what a hope. Anyway I did manage to pick it all up with a bit of luck, and happy to find my way back to our unit before it got dark. You see, it's always me if anything special is to be done. (I sometimes wished I could change my name). Still, I'm glad to say that all through my time I was able to do any job given to me. I never had to rely on anyone else to see me through.

Now we set off, first of all to build a POW cage right in the heart of the Golan Heights. The whole company goes. Our three ton lorry has three tons of barbed wire, and fourteen men as well on board. And one time, on our way up the hills the driver had to get round a hairpin bend in two locks. This was a bit gruesome for it was almost a sheer drop on one side. When we finally arrived at the place for the POW camp, it was work and no stopping until the job was done, about thirty hours or so.

There was a bit of a barrack building a distance away where our cooks were operating and I was up there at this particular time to collect the tea etc for my section when in walks a fellow, (I was sitting looking down at the floor until they had it ready). This chap said, "I just looked in to see if there was a drink of tea about". I suddenly thought "I know that accent", looked up and he said "I know you – well I'm buggered, fancy meeting you in a god forsaken place like this." The very last place on earth I expected to meet someone I knew - it was Bob Booker. I saw him once after the war, in Campden. He married a Maltese girl, so I suppose he is still in Malta now. I don't think any of his family are about Campden now.

Anyway we finished the job and went back to our old camp, collected up the other gear and went to make the road up where it had been blown away. My section had two to do on this mountain road almost opposite "Sidon". Our HQ was now at Tyre. The top blast was my particular one. It looked one hell of a job to do. We worked from six-thirty am till midnight (you could see by starlight) until the job was done. Compressors working continuously, drills and spades loosening and lifting the rock. Shale etc making a shelf in the bank below road level to build up the rock etc. You see no heavy stuff could get through until we had made a way. This was in one of the black spots of the Middle East, for malaria and sand fly fever. I was loaded with malaria and dysentery. (I shall never forget this, how I made myself go until the job was done) and to cap it all my officer came up to my job pleading and begging me to go down to the bottom job and put them right. There was him in charge, also a full Sergeant and L/Sergeant. I cursed them all to eternity but went and worked like hell, to get it moving the proper way. Then I staggered off like someone drunk towards the latrine to try and get a little relief.

When this job was done we had to move forward to a collapsed bridge. This was on the coast road towards Beirut. The bridge over the river had been blown so we had to repair this.

The Australian engineers had thrown a light bridge over it at a lower level, to get the wagons through. This was before our arrival. (By the way the Cheshire Regt. was in the hills round about, while we were on the road blow outs. They were often shooting. So we were close). I must add here that we had no water cart and no mosquito nets. We had only our bottles and cooking dixies to hold water. We had to catch the Infantry water carts, as they came back to fill up, and to let us have what was left in their water carts. This was lukewarm and horrible. On our way up to the bridge job we passed a water point. So after we had unloaded our two wagons I told one to go back and fill up our pots and pans, and what do you think? Our officer rushed up and asked where the truck was going. I told him I was sending him for water as we had nothing left. The swine said to me "No wheel will turn unless I say so". I said, "All right what is the use of me holding a rank if I can't use it, you've got to send for water or else no tea and no evening meal". This was an officer who Sam Manners Sgt., blast his soul in hell, spoilt with his stupid ways, he had come to us quite new and green. One day, later on, this officer's batman had been asleep in the officer's bed and was nearly caught out when he came up to camp for his meal. This batman just grabs a piece of greasy looking bully beef and a couple of biscuits and takes it to the officer on a plate.

Of course it was very hot now (end of June) and we had no cover except the officer who had a tent. We ate and slept out on the ground anywhere. Now this officer went off the

Middle East c.1942

deep end, when he was served like that. He later came to me like a bull in a fury, and said "In future you will look after my meals". That to me was the bitter end. I gave him the works and told him that was something I would never do. "I do all the section's dirty and difficult jobs as it is. You can go to hell from now on". You can tell what the conditions were like. When we went back to our base, I had only twenty two men left, I took fifty seven out. No one was allowed to go sick. This was an order by our OC, but naturally when fellows became really ill they held up ambulances on their way back, and so got away to get medical attention. I could have done the same.

   During those days I used to ask the sentry where the fellow was who would be on guard next in the early hours of the morning. Put a marker there and told him to get off and lie down. I'd watch the camp and call the other man at the right time. You see at that time I never slept more than an hour and a half any night. I will not give the reason here for it would take a long time to explain. The men to be on guard duty finished work at six pm, got ready and went on duty at eight thirty pm till six am. They had to report at nine am for work, so they did not get much rest.

   I had a two-gallon enamel bucket with me in which I had clean water for each morning wash and shave. Others could use it after me, but the last must clean it out and bring me fresh water for the next use. I liked to be well organized. It was my motto. About three am I used to go over to a cave where our cooks operated, light the fire and make a hand-bowl full of tea. Have a mug for myself and a drop of hot water for a shave. Then take the tea to the truck where the cooks were, get them on their feet and say "the fire is going – move! Don't let me have to come back to you". I'd then get cleaned up and lay on my blanket until it was about half five. Then I'd lug the guard onto his feet and see him on his way to wake up our chaps. Breakfast at six, parade for work at six thirty.

Chapter Thirteen
Period of Sickness

After returning to our depot we had to do a spell of refresher training. I took the whole company a section at a time going through all form of rope ties, lashing and splicing, bridging with rope ties only. At this time I was nearly done with malaria. I kept wandering for I was in a high fever. Anyway my officer was in the class to learn about ropes etc, and one morning about twenty to twelve I asked him if I could break the class off. There were only twenty minutes to go, to end of session but the (B) said, "You can have two minutes break for a smoke then carry on." That's the man he was. He knew I was near gone, and he could have at least let the chaps mess about with their ropes for that time and let me away. Now after we were finished I staggered all over the place like a drunken man, then lay down on my bed on the floor of my tent.

Our Day Sgt. was in my place and when he saw the state I was in he went to the OC and told him I must go sick. So he gave the order for a fifteen-hundred-weight truck to take me to the nearest CCS. They put me on and I nearly fell off the other side. As I said before no one could go sick, unless the OC said so. I was told later that when they rolled up my bed a black snake was there. Nice thought!

This CCS was Australian manned, so much easier and friendlier than British hospital life. CCS means 'Casualty Clearing Station'.

I had a couple of bad shivers while there and this Australian doctor said, "If you have another like that I shall send you home" But instead I was sent back as a stretcher case. First we stopped at Haifa, where in a building I was carried up three flights of stairs on the stretcher. In the morning we moved again, but this time I walked down the stairs, I could not let the chaps carry me down.

Well we finally arrived at a General Hospital at Jerusalem, where after I had recovered from this malaria I was able to get out every afternoon, but I had to wear hospital blue. Of course, it was because of my rank and a word here and there to a Specialist who looked after me, that I was able to be out so much.

Usually I used to go to one of the gates into the native quarter (Jaffa Gate), get hold of a native boy and for a copper or two he'd take me everywhere. This was at first, it was easier than roaming about, finding out places. Later, I went on my own.

The Church of all Nations is supposed to be built on the Rock which split (one could put your hand into an aperture and feel the split). This was the spot where the crucifixion took place. There were jewels of every description. All in a case, at this spot, and the Russian gift which was in a domed glass case, with the Virgin and Child in miniature was loaded with jewels worth they said £200,000, I could well believe it too. I had never seen anything like it. I walked over the paved track where Christ was supposed to carry his cross, on his way to the Crucifixion, it's all uphill.

There is a place with a hand mark in the wall, where he was supposed to have rested, on his way up. There was the Garden of Gethsemanie below, and the Mount of Olives further back. While in this particular part, I did get into the grounds of the Mosque of Omar, but no further. I was desecrating the place, so I moved on. I would liked to have seen inside, I bet it was fabulous.

While we were in Jerusalem, there was a fete at the Governor's residence. A certain number of hospital patients were allowed to go, all very nice, but very high brow. We saw the two sisters of King Farouk, they were dressed in national costume and loaded with jewellery.

During this spell in hospital, I was having treatment to try to make me sleep. They did manage to make me have about four hours. In the end the Specialist said to me – his very words "Grove, I think you ought to have a Medical Board and be graded a stage lower, and then you won't have to go into the front line". I very pointedly told him we were a working company. I wanted to be fit and I wanted to get back to my unit. Did he think a medical board would cure me? I wanted to stay A1. In the end I had to go before this Board, Colonels and Majors, four of them. They graded me B1 and this time I was in a fair wack.

I was very rude to them and said things which anyone else would have been in trouble over. However, I got over it without any trouble. I quite expected to be charged but it was all right. I did tell them that there was a cure and that I would find it. Here I decided that I would give myself to the sun whenever possible.

When I got back to my unit I did do this whenever possible.

M.P.G. BASRA c1943

Chapter Fourteen
Back to my Unit

We did work of all kinds, often using a lot of native labour, cleared specific areas in the desert to form temporary runways. We also did a tremendous amount at Aleppo. That's well up in Syria. Buildings to go up and an extension to the runway to take big planes later. This was being done by Arab contractors. I was Boss Super over this. Had to see it was done properly. All done by hand, men placing the stone patching, others blinding the surface. The contractor, a huge fellow, came to me one day and offered me quite a wad of rolled up £1 Egyptian money. Same value then as our £1. I would have none of it, then he said he would send a car for me in the evening to take me to dinner with him. He of course was trying to bribe me into letting the work pass. It was very poor work just then. I told him nothing doing, and next day I had a whole strip taken up and re-laid. That cost him a bit. I was more concerned about having a good job done, to safeguard the heavy planes which would land on it.

Oh and I did a big drain scheme on the south camp there. Opposite side of the aerodrome. All the pipes etc. for the job were made in Aleppo which was the town eight kilometres away. I used to take six native gangs and six native wagons on Sundays collecting pipes etc. also cement. There was a car to carry me around, it was held together with plates and bolts. I dare not put a load on him, but as he was allotted to the job, I made the best use of him. I had a lot of ground to check over each day, and I had a way with these natives, and got the best out of them.

After this job was finished, I had a job to do at a place called Djarra. It was an airfield near to the Turkish border. I took thirty native masons and their labourers, and about the same number of carpenters and mates, with their own transport, bedding and rations. One wagon went back to Aleppo each week to draw their rations from their own place. The chief native Boss man went with the wagon, also they called at my unit for stuff for myself. Now I was entirely on my own with these people. No other white men there.

The Australian field engineers had sunk a well and put a pump and engine unit over the hole on a couple of baulks of timber. I had to straighten it up, put a concrete base and build a pump house around the pump, roof as well. They had fixed up water storage tanks. So another job was to work the pump and fill up the tanks also purify the drinking water. There were several stone shelters to build around the perimeter to shield planes when down.

Five hundred pound bombs were put in sunken pits in the runway and covered over after. These were to blow up the runway if the enemy came through Turkey as was expected. I employed everyone who could work, from the village. All I wore at this time was a pair of gym nicks and sand shoes. Oh yes I was as brown as mahogany and felt fit as a fiddle. The men were billeted in solid buildings. I had a special place to myself with a shower-building just nearby. I used to finish work about or between five and six pm have a shower and eat my biscuits and what else there was. I frequently went to the men's place after and had a game of chequers with them. Once or twice in good moonlight they put on a sort of floor-show and put me in the place of honour and then went into their routine of Sword Dances (with sticks of course). I did enjoy this for one or two of them gave a first class show.

One Saturday afternoon a company of West African native troops arrived. They were to guard the place after we had gone. I was a bit late getting in and when I went to get my shower the place was full of naked Africans. This was the officers' place. Of course they had used all the water and began to mouth me about it. I gave them a bad few minute's talk, and told them to get out of my sight and not come in this place again. I had to explain to their officers that the water was scarce and that I had to pump it, and that they would have to be careful or the well might dry up. What finally did me, I'd have to go out to the pump about half a mile away to get a head of water in the tank for I could not wash until I had. There my luck ran out. When I started up the engine the start wheel handle would not slip off the spindle and it whipped round and banged my shins. I thought it was broken and I could not move or make anyone hear my calls. I was stuck there for three hours before I could manage to crawl away (I'll never forget that). However I got over it and when our job was done we all came back to Aleppo.

During this period, our Company was split up a good deal doing work all over the place. Some had jobs just controlling native labour. We went off on several occasions, once to a job at "Hama" airfield. In the river there was some wonderful ancient water wheels. Tremendous long arms from the hub which in itself was high, moaning and groaning as they turned, picking up water and putting it into a high aqueduct. I said they were one of the Seven Wonders of the World. They certainly impressed me.

The people in this place were not friendly and we carried arms at all times. Another time we did work at Quiser airfield, also at Homs, this was in June 1942. I have the actual movement order, connected with making a new fair-weather runway at Forgloss near Homs. All these places mentioned are in Syria. You see once again it was I who had to see to everything and collect the rations as well. I have the list of these, also other information as well as the duplicate copies of my daily report in my field book concerning the works. They are actual official papers.

The officers mentioned in the movement order. Sgt. Collinge of No.1 section and Sgt. Fox of No.2 were very good men. "Freddie" Fox as I always called him, was billeted at Blockley in the Green Howards when they were round here early in the war, he later was transferred, and commissioned in the Royal Engineers. In the end he became Second in Command. He was transport officer at first. Three times this officer arranged for me to have a complete course driving all sorts of vehicles. But it never came off. Each time I was put on to work which made it impossible. It was fate I suppose but I was still hoping. Thinking about names our officers had the following surnames, Shutt, Kay, and Fox.

One day before that last job at Forglass the OC called me into his place and told me officially to move out of No 4 section, (I had been in No.4 all the time since joining) and put myself into No 1 section. He said do it immediately. He told me later why. It seemed that No. 4 section was being sent back to base at Ismalia [*Ismailia*], Egypt. There they were to join up with a Syrian company to train and work with them, my OC said I want you here. Good, I thought at last, the Officer and Sgt. Manners are gone. Both of these were bad hats, the kind of men who could without a further thought get their men killed. So useless they were.

Chapter Fifteen
Aleppo Airfield and surrounding area

We are now back at Aleppo Airfield, billeted in good solid buildings, as seniors are in what would in civil life be married quarters. We are doing a fairish job building advanced headquarters for the RAF. This is in big chalk caves, on the outskirts of the town. This was to be ready in case the Germans came through Turkey to attack. Actually if he was powerful enough he could come through Syria, Palestine and Sinai into Egypt and join up with his forces in North Africa for they came close to it at one time in Alamein. It was possible and would have been amen to us all here.

However to get back to the work in the caves. One day the CRE suggested doing the RAF wings in stone and fixing it in the wall of the control room where the Chief of Staff would be, but who to do it? Of course our OC said "I've got the very man" The job was then ours. I had to go and see the manager of the "West African Trading Company" who controlled most civilian activities to obtain a suitable piece of stone. We settled for a piece 60x60 cms. Quite nice clear stone. This I had collected and set up on a big box in the spare room at the place where I was billeted. I had a few tools of my own and our blacksmith made one or two to my requirements out of old files and rasps. Then I set to work in all spare time. But I did more than just the RAF wings. I did the RE Badge on top, being Senior Regt. with the Wings under. When it was done they had an Official laying ceremony using a polished trowel and hammer, and declared this work well and truly laid, called for the Sculptor and said their piece. Then opened bottles of beers for the boys. This was another pat on the back for me.

Also while we were here a shooting match was arranged. Everyone in so many rounds at various ranges and a group of five shots with the Bren gun. I was able to win this contest and my five shot group with the Bren gun could have been on a penny. Our OC was on a stage giving out the results and said "I knew the Marines would do it". He knew of course that I had been a marine.

Around about this time I had a job running all the works on the airfield. This involved moving round a good deal. There was a truck with the job. And our transport officer (Freddie Fox) gave me a driver for one week, and also for me to learn to drive in that time. Well it took me all the first day to go round and get used to the job and see about requirements. I did drive it twice round but not enough to know what I was doing. I could scarcely believe it when the next day the CRE (Commander Royal Engineers) had this truck taken away. He was going to have it converted into a caravan for himself for crossing the desert. This was the first hint we had that it looked like we were going somewhere. This meant that I had lost another chance to learn to drive, for they sent another truck with its own driver. So I must not touch it, just tell the driver where to go.

As a company, during the last eighteen months we had been split up one or two here and there looking after native labour and sections miles apart. Now we have the signal, all parts of the company to report to a spot at 'Rayak' [*Rayaq*].

When I got in, late in the day, the OC had told the CQMG to break open the Company's rum issue and give the boys a welcome together drink. So soon as I showed my face the QM said, "I've been waiting for you to arrive. Show the boys how they drink the 'rum issue' in the Navy". Well he filled the Army issue enamel mug with this rum, straight out of the jar. There was only one way for me to do this, to keep faith, I just laid the lip of the mug on my tongue and quietly poured down my throat. Never again would I do it. I slipped off as soon as I could and got to bed. I must have sweated most of it out for I was all right in the morning. One of the others tried it, but went into the mess afterwards and had other drinks. He was really bad in bed for two days. Of course we covered for him.

Chapter Sixteen
Movement to Iraq

After a few days comes the order, we are going to cross the desert and go to Basra. (Top of the Persian Gulf). We load up all our kit on the wagons. The Sergeant Major says no bedding or mattresses will go, only blankets. I laughed at him and said "what about yours? He said he was entitled to take his. Fair enough I thought. Now I had a grand set up for moving about, a good sheet, a nice thin mattress and blankets all made up ready to roll up and a long thin line to secure it.

Two other sergeants asked to come in on my package, so with mine laid out, the other two beds laid on top and the whole rolled up tight and lashed with my rope we put it on my truck.

The transport went on to the collecting point. We travelled by train, Sunday midnight November 15th. Passing through Damascus, arriving at Mafraq, Monday 16th. It was very stormy here. Israeli buses arrive ready to carry us across. We are allotted our buses and on Wednesday the 18th we load up early. I have retrieved our bedding off the wagons and my bucket, these we wedge into the bus doorway, after the men are in. Then off we go at six am in convoy across the desert. The distance that day was 127 miles, stopping for the day at 3.30pm. There are no roads here just desert, so you can bet the journey is a rough affair. Of course, the first thing I do when we stop is get our bedding out of the bus, open it out and lay out our three beds near the door. Then get water in my bucket, and have a good wash. The drill being that anyone else can use it after me, but the last one must clean the bucket and fill it ready for moving, this happens every stop. We did 138 miles this day. There are 800 vehicles in this convoy.

On Friday 20th we leave at 6.30am, and because of the terrible amount of dust caused, the convoy spread out into a long line side by side. This looked tremendous. It kept us more or less free of dust as it fanned behind us, but they had to get back in line after a while, in Proper Convoy. We stopped at 5.30 pm, having travelled 146 miles this day.

As we have been travelling east, time was advanced for one hour. On Saturday we left at 9.00 am, went through Ramadi, across the Euphrates River at 12.30 and arrived at Habanya [*Habbaniya*] at 1.30 p.m. 65 miles. There was a big lake here, so we had a good swim and clean up. There was a notice post here which read London 3728 miles.

Sunday we left at 7.30 am and arrived just outside Baghdad at 11.30 a.m. We were now 650 miles on from Mafraq where the convoy began. We were given a meal here, a lump of bread and Bully and a mug of tea, I don't remember when we had bread before. It was really laughable just then, for there were lots of kite hawks overhead and they would swoop down and grab anything. One came down and took a whole piece of bread out of one chap's hands in his claws. Quite a shock for him. Lucky he was able to get some more.

We then moved on and went to Baghdad railway station where we boarded a train and left at 2.30 p.m. arriving in Basra at 9.30a.m on Monday. Naturally, we left the buses behind at Basra. They went back. We are moved from the railway in wagons to an island in the River Shatt-el-Arab just about the docks area. We have to use a pontoon bridge to go over. There is nothing on the island so we have to put our beds down where we are. Later tents are provided and in a couple of days we are organised. This is November and during the night while we are in the open we find our blankets soaking wet with dew in the morning, but hot and dry by day.

We discover our job is to build a road and rail bridge from Basra on to the island then to the other side. This was on the life-line to Persia. This is a big job. The river is very deep and fast flowing. We were driving 12"x12" teak piles up to 80 feet long with steam pile drivers, it looked like a forest of timber in the river. There were all the cross braces and runners to bolt on.

My first job there was to go to the docks and measure up all the timber, which had been stored there for this job. I measured 244,000 odd cubic feet of 12"x12" teak. Also miles of 12"x4", 6"x4" and other timber. This must have been worth a fortune. I fixed up a work place, (a wagon sheet on four posts) to give me shelter from the sun etc., as I was doing all the splicing and making steel piling bonds. To splice steel rope is no joke. Also every man working on the bridge had to wear a lifeline as we lost two or three men in the river. Once in the fast current this soon had them beat. I once went in and had to fight like hell to get out.

I discovered in the evening that big fish came up the river to feed. I could see their shadows when I stood on the timber at the edge of the bridge. This made me think. I had a forge in my work place and I took a length of 3/8" reinforcing steel, heated one end and hammered it into a spear shape, nice and thin, filed just right. Tempered it and at about 7'6" long made a ring. I fixed the end of my line to this and in the evening I quietly wandered off with it. I fixed the other end of the line to my left wrist and coiled the line and held it in the same hand. Then when I was in position I had the spear poised and managed to spear three good fish. I was tickled pink about this. I took these to the officer's mess. They had a grand feed next day. The next night I fished for our mess. This time I caught five and I must say they looked fine hanging up in our mess hut.

Soon we had some rough framework built across to one side from our island. And now work went on at a faster pace as we had better foothold. There was all the decking to bolt down and side parapets to form. Then the work began on the other side of the island. Here was a more difficult job as we had to form a drop span worked by windlass. This was to lower a section under the river to let barges and local boats through. This meant sinking steel caissons to the river bed both sides of the span filling with stone and concrete forming the bridge on each side of the span and with the drop section all fitted up and geared. During this work we saw one or two native dhows come down this side of the island, sails only (no other power) unable to control their boats they just crashed into the bridge and sank.

A railway construction company came along and laid the track from Basra over the bridge and up the Persian country on the life-line to Russia. Before our work was completed, train-loads of stores were going through with Russian guards aboard. This of course was a fair bit later sometime in June 1943.

Chapter Seventeen
A personal episode

In the meantime there was another hue and cry. A single handed job. To work on a piece of black marble for the Iraqi state railway. Once again our OC stuck his chest out and said, "I've got the very man". General Palmer at Baghdad said "to send him up with some tools". Well I had one or two more small ones made. I was ready to go and as well as all my own stuff, they, (CRE) Basra, placed in my care two trunks full of stuff to be delivered to certain officers' houses in Baghdad. Anyway we put it all on the train and off I went, where I arrived at Baghdad next station. I found that a station-wagon from CRE met all trains, this was routine. So I went in it. The driver was an Indian corporal. He took me to HQ. There I met Major-General Palmer, chief of all engineers in that part of the world (actually, he was our CRE when we were in France). He was a splendid man, we talked, and he asked a lot of questions and told me he knew my part of the Cotswolds very well and had holidays nearby. He then told his Sgt. Major to take me to somewhere to live and also a mess to feed at. This was in the morning, after which I was to take the station wagon and deliver the two trunks, then have a look round Baghdad, to get acquainted with the place, but be sure the Indian driver brought the car back when I had done with it. I had to see him again in the morning after breakfast, when he told me what the job was. It was a black marble slab that had been prepared as a foundation stone, but the chief at the railway who was going to perform the ceremony had died. So the arrangement was postponed, and now was to be prepared and re-lettered as an opening ceremony stone, at the new railway station at Mosul.

He told me to go to the railway headquarters and meet the hands there. They would put me right as to what was required. They were very friendly to me and took me to their homes, there on the railway. Very nice too. Native servants did all the work. They had a good life that I could see. Now I had this stone taken to the railway workshops where the manager had a special tool made, and with the stone on a traversing bed, this machine tool cut a narrow slice of paper thickness with each traverse and it took eight hours to groove the surface once. I had to go over it several times to clear off the old work. Then a fine polisher to follow. It was then taken to the place where I was going to work on it, and put on a stand. Now it was up to me. While I was at work there I was visited by the Prince Regent and the Prince Faisal, he was only nine years old then. So the prince ruled the state. They shook hands and we had a good chat.

When they went about in their big car there were about five outriders on motor cycles. All quite impressive. (Of course they were murdered a few years later in the state's uprising).

I completed my job and have a rubbing of it at home [Now lost. Ed]. I stayed there a fortnight. Could have hung about but thought I had better see about getting back to Basra.

The next bit has always intrigued me. I went to see the General, and told him that I was finished and ready to go back. Then he asked me if I could be ready to leave on the 6.30 evening train. Of course I said yes. Then he said "Go and say goodbye to your railway friends, then arrange a taxi to take you to the station, see the RTO Major there who will fix you up on the train". He said "he was going to Basra on that train and would see me later".

Before I go any further I ought to say that, while in Baghdad I made life for myself very pleasant, in the morning I'd get ready, walk to the mess where I was feeding round about 8.00 for breakfast then wander along to the railway HQ, probably have a chat with one or two of the staff.

There was one who originally came from Russia. He told me a good deal of what went on in his country and said he would never go back there. He spoke excellent English.

I then got down to work until about 12.00 midday or just a bit after. I would arrive back at my mess and have the midday meal. Then quietly go for a look at the place. You can tell by this that I did my job in a very leisurely fashion. After all I was my own boss and afterwards when I thought about the whole incident I considered I'd had VIP treatment.

Now to get back to my departure from Baghdad. I picked up a taxi and with my kit on board went to the station, on arrival at the entrance I nodded to a big Arab to get my gear and follow me. I paid off the taxi. This Arab spread a big blanket affair on the paving and loaded all my stuff, rifle, tools, equipment and kitbag on to it, grabbed hold of the corner and swung the lot up on to his back. Now this was a heavy load for the ordinary native to carry at once but he seemed quite happy and came after me. I found the RTO, he was a Major and told him who I was. He then told me that General Palmer had rung him and asked him to reserve a place for me on the 6.30 train. He led me down the train which was standing there and finally put me into a Reserved second class sleeper compartment and asked me if that was all right. I thanked him a lot and off he went.

Now my native put all my things into the compartment, very tidy. I gave him a broad smile and one or two "ackers" and off he went.

The train had not been travelling very long before the General came along. "Ah" he said "are you comfortable there?" naturally I thanked him for everything. He then said "I will see you at dinner, come with the first call". So later when the restaurant attendant came along calling out, "Dinner is served" I went forward to the dining saloon. I felt a bit of a clot going to sit with a General. However he made me go to his table so I was stuck with it.

He was very decent to me. No officer humbug and when the meal was over, as I left he said "See you at breakfast". Well, well

I thought. This is something out of the book.

In the morning at breakfast he asked me if I had made any arrangements for transport to take me to my unit. I said no, as how could I have done, I'd no means of contact. He then told me that a car would be there at Basra to take him to HQ and I was to get my things out by the station steps and show myself to the driver. He would return in about a quarter of an hour and pick me up. Now once more I thought this was wonderful. I thought then what other officer would have troubled to do that for me? (The usual thing is find your own way). Well sure enough this car comes back. I get in it, and with the General's flag flying on it off we went. There were police and others busy saluting, all along the streets etc., and when this car goes over the Pontoon bridge on to the island where we are living, there was a general stampede. They thought the General himself was here on an unscheduled visit. You can bet a howl went up when they saw me.

Again I say that was a tremendous period for me. Still I thought it was a sort of feather in the cap of the unit, being able to supply such varied works. Of course what I had done was a very tiny speck, but it was especially done for the Prince Regent of Iraq.

I also carved inscriptions in teak wood for two officers who had lost their lives.

On looking up my notes I find this job to Baghdad came before the time I went fish spearing. Actually I went on January twenty sixth 1943.

Chapter Eighteen
Back with my Unit

Now to get back to where the Russians were bringing trains over the bridge; some time before this, the flood water was coming down the river. You see the Euphrates and Tigris Rivers start in the mountains in Turkey and bring flood water when the snow melts in the hills. These rivers join together about thirty miles up from Basra. So by June it's in full spate and dirty too. This stopped fishing at once.

We were now living on the bottom half of the island and this part flooded badly too. We had to whip up our tents etc in a hurry and go on to the top half. It was ok there. But we did look funny sitting at our mess table for our last meal there. The water was just below our knees. Now as it was getting very hot I drove some timber into the water and made myself a duck board on top. This was in two levels so that I could be above the water but handy to it. Whenever I was not working I'd still get my bucket which I used to dip in the water and pour it over me. Of course our other seniors used it as well, in fact I have a snap or two of us. These, I hope can be produced and go with this. [Now lost. Ed.]

As our bridge job is about over there are jobs to do on the mainland. My first was to build and complete an officers' mess. We went to work at seven am, calling to leave any sick chaps for the doctor. There was a colonnade in front on the side away from the sun. One would think it would be cool there but we used to look at the thermometer hanging there in the shade, and it read ninety-seven, at seven regularly. And by one o'clock it was one hundred and thirty in the shade. Later came the date winds. They blew a hot humid wind which made the dates change colour. They ripened during that time. This took some standing too but we were by now tough.

Another job was a special cool room for the second stretcher staff. Poor things, we had no comfort that way, just tents. By the way the river at this lower point was called the "Shatt-el-Arab", it was also tidal water. The docks being down river about a mile from our island. Being tidal water made it worse for flooding our island. Our bridge was called the Shatt el Arab Bridge.

During August our OC Major Tom Cox was promoted to Lt.Colonel and of course left us to take over another CRE. So our Second in Command gets promoted to Major Shutt, and we have a Captain Kay as second at this time. I was full Sgt. but following incidents soon made a difference. We were at this time full strength. I, being Boss of No.3 section. This was because our old Sergeant Major had to leave our unit, owing to his drunken state. The officers got him away. He was posted to a Transit Camp where after a while he managed to get in charge as Sgt. Major, and now, to spite our outfit, he posted to us, from his camp, two full Sergeants. We did not want them but had to accept them. Now one of these had been full rank longer than I, so he took my place and I had to climb down, losing my bomb-badge. The other fellow had to go down a rank, as he too had not had his rank as long as the rest. Our new OC was livid but could do nothing about it.

Now, the time has come for us to move again. I have been detailed to go with Lt. Freddie Fox to take all our transport out from Basra, and across the desert, right into Egypt. I have a party of six sappers to do guard duties when we are halted for the night. These Arab races are very clever at stealing as I well knew. So extreme alertness was the order.

Chapter Nineteen
Journey to Egypt

We left Coal Island, Basra at 4.20 am on September 1st 1943 and arrived at Ur at 1.00 pm, distance 130 miles. That was our scheduled stop. One tent was put up for the officer, I used it as well, and slept in it. That was Wednesday. Next morning we moved out at 4.00 am, and arrived at Khan Jadwah at 12.30 midday. This was Thursday and 120 miles travelled. You notice we were going in easy stages but this helped the driver, as it gets very monotonous, driving in the heat, and this time there is a proper tarmac road, and the fumes that rise from it in the heat are very nauseating. Of course there is a water point at each stop, which is a good thing and also by starting early we escape some of the worst of the heat.

Here it is Friday and we leave Jadwah at 3.50 am. arriving at our next stop just outside Baghdad at 10.00 am. This time only 96 miles. We stay here until Sunday the fifth when we left at 5.30 am and arrived at stage 1 at 4.30 pm. This was 120 miles. On Monday we left stage 1 at 4.45 am and arrived at stage 2, Rutbah at 2.30 pm, distance 140 miles. Tuesday we left Rutbah at 5.00 am arriving at stage 3 at 1.30 pm a distance of 130 miles.

During this journey one frequently saw mirages. I remember once there were in the distance a herd of camels. They seemed to grow taller and finally it looked like a beautiful city, with tall minarets, surrounded by clear blue water. Quite an unbelievable sight. Often one saw heat haze changing into fantastic shapes. Next day we left at 5.30 am arriving at Mafraq at 12.50 pm, 127 miles. Next day we left at 6.30 am and went through the Jordan pass, arriving at Tulkarm at 16.45 hrs. This was 122 miles. Friday the 11th we leave at 5.50 am and arrive at Asliy [*Asluj*]. This is just in the Sinai desert, at 2 pm, 128 miles.

Of course all this time I have to keep a sharp look out in case of breakdown, or anyone not keeping in his proper position.

There must not be any crowding or long gaps.

This is familiar country to me as I stopped at this point when we first crossed this desert on our way to Palestine and Syria. We have a good wash and clean up here, for there is plenty of sand and dust always in this country.

We leave here at six o'clock on Saturday, cross the Sinai and arrive at Qantara at 6.00 pm. This was 170 miles. We crossed the canal at 6.15 pm same day and arrived at 153 transit camp at 7 pm. Ten miles. We left here at 10.30 am Sunday September 12th and arrived at Qassasin camp at 12 o'clock only 28 miles this time. This was also the end of our journey across the desert, a total distance of 1321 miles.

Here we join our unit who came by rail. You see now there is road and rail across the desert. Next we went to a ferry point on the canal for one week, bridging, and from there suddenly we were loaded into transport and taken to a camp on the outskirts of Mena. This is where the Pyramids are. Here we have to go to various private houses and areas nearby to do the defences for the Mena Conference.

Chapter Twenty
Back to work and a meeting with Churchill

My job with my section was the defences at Spink House. This is the house where Winston Churchill stayed. Quite a lot of meetings were held in this place between him and top generals and admirals. There were British detectives about as well as marines posted at the gateway which led from the house. These houses are built round a square courtyard open to the sky, only one storey with doors opening on to the courtyard. We all had to carry special passes. [*Now lost Ed.*]

We booby-trapped the grounds but that did not work as they were set very lightly and the change from heat to chill in evening time caused the wires to tighten just enough to set them off. There were bangs everywhere at night. Now this was no good at all. Could very well upset old "Winnie". Oh yes, dogs as well caused them to blow up. So we cleared them away.

Outside the grounds we had put three coils of barbed wire all round the perimeter, and the roadside as well. Now because of this conference there were tanks and armoured vehicles roaming about, and planes too. One morning a tank came down the road and managed to hook his track in the barbed wire and in no time he had torn about a quarter of a mile of this three coil stuff after him before he was stopped. This was quite a mess and took some sorting out, but we put it back ok.

By the way I saw President Roosevelt, he was moved about in a wheel chair. In fact I saw about all who were at this conference, including Chiang Kai-shek.

Now in the centre of the courtyard at Spink House there was a nice old antique marble statue (quite small) standing in a small pond or fountain. This figure sent a jet of water up as high as fourteen feet when it was turned full on. There was a control on one wall. Now Winnie used to like to mess with this in the evening. I should think it soothed his tiredness. Anyhow one day he bawled out for his secretary who dashed out of a room on the other side, forgot in his haste all about the fountain and plunged straight at it. Naturally broke it up quite a bit.

There was now another hue and cry. It must be repaired at once. Yes you've guessed it was me again. But I said "I will have to get into Cairo into the Suq (market) to get what I want", I wanted to anneal it. Sort of sweat it together with gentle heat from a blow lamp and certain crystals which I have forgotten all about now. That was late in 1943. While I was doing this marble repair Winston Churchill came up to me on two occasions with a little chat each time. In the end he said, "I hope you will be able to repair it". I told him I was very confident I could. I did speak to him about married men being kept so far away and so long from home but there was nothing doing.

While we were in this area I, with others, went to the pyramids and got into the King's Chamber as they called it. There I noticed a polished granite slab nearly the width of the place. I reckoned about 15'x7'6". There seemed to be no mortar joint but the fit was perfect. They certainly had tools in those far off times. Then there was the old Sphinx. Sedately squat there looking over the Nile area. Actually in olden times the river used to flood and reach up to this place, when the rains came at the source of the river. This makes the Nile Delta very fertile, thouands of years of silt from floods.

As soon as the conference is over we all clear off again. We went next to near Suez on December 9th to prepare a campsite for 20,000 troops. This was a rush job, in fact they were arriving while we were still there. Their white faces and legs looked funny to us for of course we were very brown. My skin was like mahogany all over. You can imagine the amount there was to do on a site for a division, all the cookhouse work, wash places and lines of latrines. In the holes of some of these you could see what looked like a powder fuse trail; in fact we could detect the burnt smell.

Now I was given a fifteen-hundred-weight truck and driver to get me about the work, as we had to push it through quickly. I logged the distance I did, one day and it was 111 kilometres. That would be somewhere about 75 miles. This camp-site must have been very near to where the latest Arab/Israeli fight ended in 1973-4. This job was finished on January 12th 1944.

We were now moved over to the Sinai side of the canal. Still down near Suez. The place was quite an area of salt flats; it was very damp sand, but firm and was easy for the vehicles. From here we had to go off a ways to build a big refugee camp for Yugoslavs, Tito's lot. This we started January 13th 1944. We had to put down 70 40'x16' concrete bases with tiles laid on top. Tents were to be erected on these bases for for dining purposes.

Then there were cookhouses and wash houses to build and of course a proper drainage system, also latrines. This was quite a job. And as well as all this we had a reinforced concrete water-tower to build. There are some miniature snaps of this. [*Now lost. Ed*]. These refugees were coming in while we were still busy and we tried to get some of the men to work with us. There was only one, a blacksmith who volunteered. We put him in a shelter to do the steel bonding for the water tower. But after a bit, he, through a camp interpreter told me he dare not work anymore as the others would set about him. They told me straight out "You brought us here. We did not want to come, and we are not going to work for you".

That was that, but on top of it all you should have seen the rations they had. Everyone, baby upwards, received one pound of lovely bread per day, plenty of meat and all the other were Australian rations. We felt very bitter as we were on biscuits, bully, sardines and some tinned stuff like say, Irish stew. Why should they have such food?

It was on this job that I caught Iricipllis. I do not know the correct spelling of this word, (Erysipelas) but enough to know that it put me in a separate tent for infectious complaints, and I was there for twelve days. Then finally the matron and sister said "you can get up today and look in the glass, have a shave, but don't cut yourself or you will have it again". This startled me, and it took a good hour before I had it done. I did not want any more of that.

Later in the year, September, we went up to Al Tira not far from Haifa, Palestine. Here we do a lot of training, hill climbs and long marches as well as taking courses in making anti-personnel bombs etc. At this time one had to check everything when you went with your tent. Clever dicks would set them up anywhere, but in this case only use detonators.

We also had odd and sods of all kinds up for training. Some naval, some police, and others who may become involved when the job comes off. The intention is to make a big raid on Cos a strongly held and fortified island in the Dodecanese.

While we are still at Tira we do a long march down the coast to an old Roman fortified area, Ceaserea [*Caesarea*]. Here we are to practice working and offloading stones etc. from a z-craft. This is a long flat bottomed boat. Well there never was such a mess. It was blowing up rough by the time the boat arrived, and she swung sideways on. There we were, stripped off, dozens of the chaps hanging on a long rope trying to hold the boat steady and turn her stern onto the beach. After hours of wasted labour, it was decided to pack it in and the boat pulled away. We then had all that way to march back.

November 12th 1944, Sunday. We pulled out of Tira and went back through Asliy, Sinai desert and Mena to Al Amriya not very far from Alexandria, stayed here a while then on Saturday December 2nd 1944 we moved again and arrived at Beni Yousif. We stayed here until after Christmas.

This was the first time the unit sat down together for a proper meal. Extras had been bought and Christmas dinner was all right. The senior NCOs and officers waited on the men.

There were proper rooms here for reading and games etc.

And it was here that I saw in the Post magazine, beautiful photographs of Westington and the almshouses and church at Campden. It made me feel like crying my eyes out. We had been away four years nearly. And that is no joke at all.

While at this place, in the afternoon when I was free, I used to walk off along the desert. Keeping near the river for positioning as without a compass and map one could quickly go astray. I came across two pyramids which I located as being at Saggara [*Sakkara*], outside were two large stone bowls with scallops in the top edge. These I am sure were for bathing. One could imagine oils and soaps in the scallops.

St James' Church and Almshouses

I could see into the entrances of the pyramids. They were going down. How I wished then that we were a party going to open them up. There were lots of excavations done in later years, and many beautiful things found. I saw some of these pictures in a *Telegraph* magazine, I still have it.

The raid on Cos gets started. The first wave go and they receive a battering from Gerry. Guns and equipment get lost in the sea while trying to offload, and in fact the whole thing is a failure. In three days we see some of the fellows we knew are now back again, so that let us out, as we were to follow as soon as the first wave had established a bridgehead.

Now I find that I have overrun my story, somewhere, for during early summer, with our HQ at the Salt Flats Camp, my section was at Fanara. This was part of GHQ Canal zone. There were various regiments' bases there. We were on jobs round about, and one day I noticed all the troops were hanging about their billets, I asked one or two what was going on, and they said "We have a day's holiday today – Kings Birthday". I thought, "Well we never have a day off not even on Sunday. Every day is the same with us". So I went smartly around and found my officer and pointed out this fact to him and said if they can have a day off what about us? He then said "Come with me, we will go and see the CRE Major". I had to go in with him to explain any case, and it was agreed we could have from midday off. Of course it did not amount to much as there was nowhere to go. The chaps just lay about, read or slept, but I had gained a point.

We of course were living in the usual tents. Soon we moved up to Fayid still in the Canal Zone. RASC and RAOC were there as I remember.

I was given the job to build a big twin Nissen hut as they called it. Quite a big place, and to be workshops. I was given a big bunch of blueprints. So we laid the concrete base first. This would give us somewhere clean to lay out the materials.

I went to the ordnance supply depot. There were all sorts there, civilians too. They told me all the stuff was there for two or three of these buildings but they had no idea what to supply. I then said "I will bring a list of items as I require them. Then each time I come for more I will return anything not needed". You see I had the prints with all the pieces shown and named. This worked out very well, and later the stores-men thanked me for everything. They now knew exactly what was required for these buildings, and strange to say, had an order to supply one more which was to be despatched by rail.

I had also some work going which involved native labour. On one job the native people came to act as guards, as this was an outlandish spot. But still thieving went on. Of course it was quite likely that some of these guards were in on the stealing. One night I thought I would walk out to the site with my rifle loaded. I would have shot anyone I caught, in the legs if possible. An example had to be made, but these Arab people live by stealing. That is, or was, their way. They are very slick and would go greased and naked if they were after anything where they might get caught. They'd be too slippery to hold. At all events as I went on my way every now and then I heard a dog let up a howl. I thought then, they are too smart for me. I bet there were youngsters placed all over the area, with or without dogs to give warning of any approach. I did not see a thing on this trip, and did not bother to go again, as it was quite a way to go, as well as being very eerie.

After a while we suddenly got the order to return to our own unit, HQ. This meant I had to tear round and get the stores and tools drawn from CRE returned and receipted and native labour dealt with, while some of our other chaps had to get the tents down, folded and tagged and returned to stores. There were these natives all sat around looking sorry for themselves, kept saying they wanted me to stay.

We loaded up and were on our way, and arrived at our HQ late, hungry and tired. Our tents were already up. So it was just a case of get in and down to it.

Now as I said before, this was all salt flats here. When I lay down I put my rifle partly under my body and pay book etc. under my head, this night I hung my shirt on the inside of the tent wall over my body, and left my watch, pen and propelling pencil in the shirt pocket. Now I was always a very light sleeper, and the thieves must have caused me to wake. The first thing I did was reach up for my shirt which was not there, then felt along the ground by my bed. No, it was not there either. So by this time I was wide awake. It was brilliant moonlight and I could see bare foot marks where an Arab had stood while going over my stuff. Of course by now my noise had awakened three other sergeants. I said, "we have been raided". They looked round and right enough they had been done. Pay books and all their money taken.

I looked outside and there about 50 yards away I saw something on the ground, and went to it, and what do you think, yes, it was my shirt. It was quite dry so could only have been there at most three minutes. Of course, all the pockets were empty. The L/Sgts' tent next to us was a real mess, things scattered everywhere. They had had a real going over. The Sgt. Major's tent was ransacked, and we later found that they had sorted out the stuff in the Officers' latrine. Papers were everywhere.

Next day we had the field security there with a tracker. They took particulars of our losses and said if they found our things they would send them on. You see we were moving next day.

At this point I return to where we left Baghdad Railway Station and moved to an Island in the River Shatt.

All the transport was loaded and lined up on the road in our camp. There was the driver and his mate sleeping on their wagons. We also had a field security Sgt. Major with a jeep attached to us, now we had a guard and guard house just at the end of the road, also there were two prowler guards walking about round the wagons. In the morning, very early, I looked around and thought, what the hell is wrong with the jeep. It was down on its belly. The Arabs had been and quietly removed all four wheels and the spare.

They have great patience, these people are either almost naked or with their drab smocks (called gallabieh) you could walk close to them and not notice them. Once a young Arab worker pointed a native out to me. He was squat, quite out in the open, late afternoon. In the ordinary way one would not notice him. You'd have to be searching. The lad said to me, "Look Sgt., bye and bye him plenty clifty", (meaning steal) that was pretty well how they lived in the open spaces.

Chapter Twenty one
Leave Egypt for The Dodecanese Islands

Now then we were moving off early as soon as the cooks had stowed their gear, and breakfast over. I forgot what happened to the jeep, but they must have managed to get more wheels from the nearest supply depot. We made for Alexandria loaded with compo boxes. You see we were off to the Dodecanese islands and had to carry all our rations for a long period. It was all in boxes, each box – ration for one for 14 days or 14 for one day. We had to load it all on to a Greek destroyer, then we all get on board and sail. After about an hour (what do you think) my section chaps asked, "can we have some tea?" Here we are, loaded on a destroyer, all that gear stacked, and they want tea. I thought, my Lord, what am I surrounded with, and I gave them the old acid.

After a few hours the ship drops anchor in a nice bay, at the island of Symi. I watched the anchor chain go down and it came to the parts painted red. Thirty-four fathoms – 204 feet down. No.2 section off loaded here, with all their kit and rations into landing craft and put ashore.

Then we up-anchored and away are again, a while later, my lot went into a z-craft and made for Kasos. Now we hit some rough weather. It's too rough to go around between Kasos and Scarpanto, so we carry on along the bottom side of the island, and out and up the other side, but its just as bad here. I could see the boat. Steel sides, grate and shudder, also some small cracks showing. I thought this will be a rum how do you do, if we get waterlogged or sink, but as well as that, there in the distance easily seen was Crete. Now that island was very strongly fortified and held by the Germans. Look well if they spot us and come after us. Anyway the skipper turns the boat round and we pull in a small cove and drop anchor.

The island stood up near vertical above us, a couple of

hundred feet for sure. There were goats on these high rocks and ledges, as we could see, when we first went by. We were ordered, no lights to show, just in case. The anchor dragged so they took it in and we had to sail, to keep off the rocks. It was most unpleasant in the night, prowling about. One almost felt like talking in a whisper in case Gerry heard us. Of course it was not like that, just a feeling, but it was two days before the water went down enough for us to approach our island.

They had only a very tiny little bay, with a narrow entrance. So, we had to make a wet landing. The craft pushed her stern in until she grounded, and then dropped the stern section and from then on we all had to carry the stuff ashore wading through 2-3 feet of water. There were plenty of journeys to make, to get all our gear, and all those boxes of rations ashore. They were our life-line.

Actually I had collared some of the Indian rations (there was a party of them on the ship) they should have looked after their stuff. I've learnt by now. Self first and always. After the z-craft had gone, we had to carry all that gear etc. up through the tiny island village, up shallow steps mostly, to a point where several empty dwellings were. Sorted a place for the cooks, and fixed the men up and ourselves in a small residence in a courtyard. It might have been the village meeting place, although they did have a mayor and a kind of market cum town hall. All business and trade was done there. The fisher folks sold their catch there, and the mayor seemed to handle all of it. In fact I have a ring with initials on, which he had made for me. I found the silver coin to make it. [Now lost. Ed.]

As soon as we were settled in, my section job was a camp for Italian refugees at a place called the fountain. There was a water point there, a stone building with a running water pipe outlet. It was a high volcanic island, and I had to measure the flow of water every day and keep a record. It was quite a walk from our camp to the job and except for a few terraced bits of ground, was like being on the moon. It was all rough volcanic.

At this Italian camp I was supposed to build out to sea, a jetty so that z-craft could come alongside and bring stores and food for the camp. There was also another one being made on the other side of the island. This was for Greek refugees. I had surveyed the shore in a boat, using a native boat with a glass bottom. This you could hold touching the water and get a good view of the bottom. Anyway it was very reasonable and flat.

I was told I would have fifty tons of cement for the job, but there was none at that time in the Middle East. The native folk said there would not be any more storms now and as they usually know these things, I had to set to work on it and build it dry.

I had all the useful men and boys at work, some with ponies carrying stone or sand. Any old buildings and rocks were collected and brought home. I used to work in the water from 9am till 4pm with some good chaps with me, who worked in relays, placing, chinking and spreading sand etc on top.

One of these was an old jail-bird who had been sent to our unit. I was good to him and looked after him. (Some of the other seniors were watching for a chance to get him for something). That was not my way at all. I warned him and made very sure he knew he had to play the game with me and I would see him right. Now this chap worked in the water with me and when I ordered him out he said "I'll go when you do". Well that was the way of it. You see he was not bad, just went wrong.

Naturally as I suppose you know the Mediterranean Sea is not tidal so we did not have trouble over that. However after we had been five days working on this jetty, I happened to look out to sea and I saw "white horses" showing on the water. I cursed it a bit, and called my lads away from the jetty as I knew what these sudden squalls could do. So as the time was getting on we slowly headed for our billets.

In the morning when we went over to the camp all our work

had been washed ashore. If it had kept steady weather the jetty would have lasted until some bridging form of structure could have been obtained and fixed up. So now all the requirements would have to come ashore, as we did. Still, that would find a job for the natives. They were soon here at the camp. All had to be "de-loused," men and young children. After they were settled in, I had all the men paraded and with the interpreter found what they could do. One was an artist, Scarpenti by name. I detailed him to paint all the camp notices etc. and to paint my portrait in particular. He did not have much of a paint selection so my portrait was not particularly good. (It is here somewhere). [Now lost. Ed.] Others were given general camp jobs and some to put up extra tents (the camp was tented), some for cook house work etc.

We had built latrines, a wash place and a cookhouse, and there was the sea to bathe in. Now I used to parade these Italians at 9am and look them over, then send them to their jobs, and do you know, there was not one to be seen in a quarter of an hour. They were all back in with their women. Some of my lads were in a state because these folk would not work. They wanted to have a go at them. Don't forget, I was mad too. We had slaved enough for them, so in the end I said to a few of our boys, "Look I've got to go over to the other side of the Island, I shall be away for a while. Now be careful, do not mark them where visible, and go for the body if you have to. But watch it. The women will be against you and might report it. So watch it." I then cleared off and left them to it. Later they told me about going in the tents and dragging these chaps out. Some were naked or near enough. The women screamed at them, but they let off some steam and I felt that it had done our lads a bit of good. There were not complaints either. So all in all, it was a good job done and the Eyeties were more prominent at work after that.

There was only my section on Kasos now. HQ and No. one

section went over to Scarpanto, a large island just two miles away. We settled down to routine work.

One day I spotted a large bundle on the shore some distance away. So I called up one of the natives who had a pony at work and we went over to it. It turned out to be a bale of brand new blankets which must have been lost from some boat or other in those parts. Anyway we brought it back, and through this find, were able to get all my section's blankets changed for these new ones. Now that was good for we had had our old ones all the time we were out, over four years. You can shake them and sit them in the sun but they are still dirty and smelly. Yes that was a good move.

I should point out here that there were only a few dozen people living on this island, it was so poor. Half the houses were empty. The folk had either gone or been destroyed. Poor devils, they had been under Turks, Greek or Italian control for years and before this they were in for it by the wandering raiding parties at the time of the Crusades. The fishermen used to go out in their small boats and use the swing-circle net style for fishing, but mostly they would use a bit of dynamite with about a half-inch fuse. I suppose they waited until they saw fish in the water, then threw the dynamite in, and I should think the shock of the explosives brought the fish to the surface so they could gather them.

One day I saw such a boat doing just that. The sound of the explosion drew my attention to him. After this I could see he was rowing for home, so I set off pretty fast and arrived at the tiny landing place, as soon as he did. He had two fine fish. Shaped like big squat goldfish. Nice colour too. I was with him all the time as he walked to the market with his catch. I kept saying, "one for me". "No" he said "Officer, Officer" "No Johnny" I said, "one for me". However when the fish were weighed with the mayor seeing to it, I said to him, "one for me", he nodded, and I was pleased to pay what he said, and take it to my mess, where we made a nice meal out of it. Quite a change from our compo rations.

Do you know, two of these fisher-folk blew themselves up, with that dangerous way of fishing? It seemed very sad, poor women with children, and now no support.

I now receive a very urgent signal. This is early one Sunday morning. I have to report at our HQ on Scarpanto, using the first boat going over. Now here was a thing. It was blowing like hell again, quite unusual for this time of year. April should be good. Anyway I got on the native caique, a sort of sailing boat, with an auxiliary engine and prop. There were also one hundred refugees on board to go to Scarpanto as well.

Now we sailed at 12 noon on what was normally a half an hour trip. As we met the weather all the refugees went to the leeside, this made the boat have a distinct list. We were all swilled with spray and the small boat being towed behind broke loose and soon smashed on the rocks. I could see us doing the same thing, but then I thought these native boatmen must know how far they can risk it, but me, I have no faith in them. Life seems cheap to them. However we did get in but not till six thirty. That was six and a half hours to do the half hour run.

I was met at the boat and taken to a tent to live in, and then saw the OC who explained what it was all about. I had to take over all the work on the island. The other section had to go and help out on Symi.

Here, a distance from our camp was a very good little harbour and landing stage, and it was decided to build two large storage buildings for refugee stores and food, to be sent from here as required. I was given the drawings and told to proceed, materials now being available here.

One evening I had just returned to camp, when a messenger came to me saying the OC wants to see you at once. He is in the officer's mess. So off I go and straight in. There he was pacing up and down, and he said, "What will you have to drink",

I told him whiskey. He seemed too full up to speak for a few minutes. Then he said "Grove, you are made up at last and back dated, so they can't take it away from you again. You are now "War Substantiated" meaning officially recognised, full sergeant" (You have to hold the rank nine months before it is so recognised). He was so glad about it and so was I. And anyway I knew I had earned it the hard way.

Now my section is called over from Kasos. It seems we are to move again, and we do so in a day or two. My storerooms construction never got off the ground. I could see the reason soon, the war was about over.

I met my section at the jetty when they came from Kasos, I was watching closely and in the end said where are your rations, come on, where are they? Do you know the B-fools had forgotten them, left them behind? (Oh my God I thought, what am I surrounded with) one officer, one L/Sgt, two corporals and cooks as well. I said, now then, how are you going to live. The first essential thing is the last you do. Very luckily for them I had luck with the quarter master. He fortunately had got hold of some extra rations so they were all right. It could have been awkward as there was no way to get back to the island, and anyway I bet the poor islanders were quickly on the scene after our men had left and anything would have vanished like the wind.

We now hear that the war is about over and we are to take over at Leros, this is a fine sea-plane base. Germans are here in full command, after the Italians gave in. We load up, with all our rations, onto a landing craft. The headquarters move out to Rhodes Island.

We sail on and the naval officer in charge of the boat quietly told me "we are going in over the minefield, but don't tell the men". I can tell you I felt a bit nervy myself. But then we are very shallow in the water so must be safe. Well we landed safely and settled in a very nice building with a big balcony which we used to parade on. This was very useful. By the way, the Navy came along in two days, sweeping up the minefield and blowing them up.

This island was certainly a very important place during the war.

Seaplanes could cover all the area, and the island was infested with concealed gun positions. There was, or had been a hospital there. The Greek Sacred regiment were just leaving as we arrived. They had rounded up all the Germans. A party of Indian troops arrived as well. They took over the job of dealing with the prisoners.

A bunch of them with a Sgt. Major in charge (Germans I mean) reported to me for jobs to do. He gave me a smart salute, which I returned, and he followed my instructions to the letter. Every job was done to perfection. Of course Germans are very thorough and no trouble.

I had the special job of going all over the island, up the cliff places, looking for any RE stores, or explosives. I was given a German jeep and driver to take me about. Some of these places were tucked in hidey-holes. Oh it seemed a thousand feet down to the water. One could see a long way around too. I never did find anything much on these trips, but they had to be done. I did not see any civilians either. It must have been a complete naval cum military fortress.

Chapter Twenty Two
War about over
Return to Egypt for Release

Now the time has come for me to leave as I am due for the next lot for release. One morning a small motor boat comes for me. So I hand over to the L/Sgt., pack my kit and say goodbye to the officers and my lads, and get on this tiny flat-topped boat. Two other sappers are with me. They are time serving and are going home for leave. Then afterwards back to their depot.

Now once or twice we had to hang on for dear life, for as we passed another island the wind seemed to rush down its side and hit the water and in a minute it was all one toss about. These motor launches were very tiny. Not so bad for the chap in the cockpit, he had a steering wheel to hold on to. We could only hang together. I was damned glad when that journey was over and we arrived on Rhodes where I reported in.

The OC told me I would be there a week before moving on. He wanted me to have a break. All I did was go to see a doctor in Rhodes for an examination, ready for release report. There were my papers to get ready and he said he was also sending me a fortnight early so that I could have leave in Alex before going home. So I just sat around quietly helping to drink all the bottles of stuff they had in the mess. It seems our SM and an artillery SM found a German store of drinks. So they shared it and got it to the mess. There were bottles all round the place.

Freddie Fox who was now our 2nd in command said to me "I shall have to find you a nice little job while you are here" and I quickly said "Freddie, you are too late, I'm doing no more". Of course he was joking.

When we do leave we have to get on the deck of a coal burning boat, a tramp steamer. By the time we got to dock we were filthy, dirty and black.

Now instead of putting in at Alex [*Alexandria*] this boat went to Port Said. There was no way back so I had to go from Port Said by train right down to Ismalia, and go to the base there, then get a new rail pass to take me back to Alex.

This was a nuisance. I did not get much food. Still when we did arrive at Alex there was transport meeting every train. They took us to the camp and found us some places to sleep. Then the chap on duty said "how about food?" I quickly told him I was starving, for I had had none at Ismailia (you see I had quite a load of kit etc. and the Sgts. mess was right at the opposite side of the depot, and for the short time I was to be there, I could not be bothered to go to it. Besides I was a bit rough. Not like the spruced up base wallahs).

The two sappers I brought from Rhodes brought me tea back from their mess.

Now the company office was just close to the hut we were in at Ismalia. I saw the clerk, showed him my papers and told him I, with the other two sappers, must get away from here today. You see, I was supposed to be on leave, before release. I gave him a pound or two and this did the trick. We were called in the afternoon and I received the railway passes and a truck was there to take us to the railway.

During that morning I made myself look a bit presentable, and then had to walk over to the other side of the camp, to change all our money. You see in the part of the world where we had been, we had to use BMM (British Military Money), which could only be spent in army canteens etc. We were in what was called Paiforce. (Persia and Iraq force.)

Now back at Alex Rest Camp, the fellow who was seeing to us on arrival took us into the cook place, produced a knife and cut off a grand piece of roast beef for each of us and with a lump of bread, we were now OK.

In the morning we showed up at the company office. I had leave papers as well as release. No.7 release group were leaving the release centre that day for England. So the OC sent me off at once to that centre. But when I reported in it was too late.

The next Group No. 8 which was my paper lot were due to leave in a fortnight. This I already knew as I had come early to have a leave here first. The camp authorities were undecided whether to send me back to the Rest Camp till I was due to go. Anyway I managed to stay, although it was very dull in this empty camp. I became very friendly with the camp Sgt. Major, and used to go about the camp quite a bit with him. He knew where to get drinks at any time. Not that I wanted it but one has to mix with what goes on.

The camp adjutant came into the mess one morning when we were having coffee there. He was all right. He said, "We shall have to find a job for you while you are here", I quickly told him, nothing doing. I'm on leave, and if I want he'd get nothing out of me. I've finished". He could only laugh, and we shook hands over it.

I did walk to the sea but it was quite a long way so I only went once.

Chapter Twenty Three
Return Journey, England and Home (Campden)

Now it's my turn to come home. We were told the ship had had engine trouble and this put us a day behind. Anyway she was stood off, away from shore, so we had to load into flat barges and go to her that way. This was very bad for us as we had to climb up the ships ladders, and in addition to this, the sides of the barges were about four foot high, and we had to carry all we possessed at one journey. There was no going back for a second load. I had got a big kit bag as well as full marching order. How we all made it I'll never know.

The ship was the "Caernarvon Castle" one of the Union Castle line which operates between Southampton and Capc Town, South Africa, a very fine ship.

As soon as we sailed the staff asked for Senior NCO's to volunteer for Police duty. I had heard a whisper so I was quickly on to it. You see, we were stacked in bunks below decks, whereas this police job put us into a big cabin right on deck level, amidships, aft. Also the cabin would not come under inspection during the trip (whereas the rest of the ship was kept spick and span). Everyone had a large ticket with all meals marked on, each time one went to eat the appropriate No. was punched, like a ticket collection job. Now it was Cafeteria feeding on this ship and the men had to come up each meal time, you could stand a long time waiting, but with us on Police duty we put on the arm band and passed right by the line, down the stairway, get the ticket punched and into the dining saloon. (In a manner of speaking one could, if it agreed with the turn of duty one was on, get a meal, do the appointed time of duty and be off while the last few were still getting fed) Really Police duty was only a matter of form. Nobody was going to be foolish enough to make trouble just at this final period before leaving the Service. We did not report to anyone either.

Once I was on duty in the Main First Class Lounge, lobby. There were ranks of all sorts up and down the stairway. Seniors only of course. It was just a simple exercise which helped to pass the time on our way home.

The ship called at Malta to pick up a few then on through the Straits of Gibraltar and so into the Bay of Biscay where the ships engines promptly broke down. Luckily for us the sea was fairly steady. If it had been rough we'd have had a bad time, with no steerage way at all.

After two days they had one engine going, and we were diverging about on a zig-zag course going very slow. Next day they had the other going, so we were able to continue our journey.

Someone must have failed to make proper contact, and arrangements at Southampton, for when we arrived it was on a Sunday, and no one knew anything about us, so had to stay on board. There were police patrolling the quayside. The boys on the ship gave them quite a going over, the usual thing, when something very familiar is seen after a long time.

When we did leave the ship we were put straight into trains. Ours went to Oxford where we were put into a Camp at Cowley for forty eight hours. Then we were taken by train again to Taunton where we handed in such equipment etc. as was required and then received our release papers and warrants etc.

By this time it was after six pm and they told me it would be better if I stayed the night there, which meant I would not be able to get a train for home that night. I told them to let me have my rail warrant and I'd get along.

We were transported to the railway station and I put my stuff in the cloaks while I had a look around. There was a young RE lad assisting the RTO on the station. We got talking and he saw my first war ribbons, and said his dad was in that war as well. Then he told me that a fast train came along and stopped at Taunton for a couple of minutes at about ten to twelve midnight and that its next stop was Reading at about four am, I think, or four twenty, and if I moved fairly quickly over to the opposite side of the station I could catch the milk and mail train to Oxford arriving about six am I think it was.

Well this sounded all right to me for I was sure I would get something from Oxford, home. I had all my stuff ready and true enough the train did come right on time. I was soon in, left my things in the corridor. The train was pretty full and everyone seemed to be sleeping. I saw a useful spot and backed myself into the seat, forced them apart, being the only way. I felt no, I'm damned if I will stand in the corridor for four hours. It looked as if all these people were coming back from holiday. It was July 27th 1945. I bet they thought I was a "darkie" when they woke up for of course I was very darkly tanned indeed.

However we did arrive at Reading on time and did get the other train. There was a Sgt. Major in the compartment. We got talking and when we arrived at Oxford I put my gear in the cloaks and went with him to a big YMCA place not far down the road where I had a good wash and clean up, and a fair breakfast, after which I wandered back to the station and caught a train which landed me at Campden about midday.

Suddenly it all seemed very strange and quiet. Then I rode up home on George Haysum's bus which seemed very quaint after all the hustle etc. Still it was marvellous to be here at last.

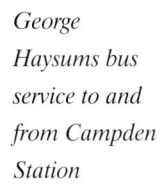

George Haysums bus service to and from Campden Station

You know I had been away four years and five months and did not recognise young Robert who was then 10 years old, and I'm sure he did not want to know me at first, why should he? I looked like a native then.

Tony was grown up so it was easier for him. In front of my dear wife I felt horribly guilty for having left her in the lurch for so long, but, at the same time proud, very, very proud that she was my wife. I had loved her with everything within me from very soon after we first met and my feelings for her have never changed. One does not often put these things on paper but in this case it is the all-important item in my life.

I still have my release papers and I think they should be with various other papers and snaps joined into this document so that the whole thing can be perpetuated.

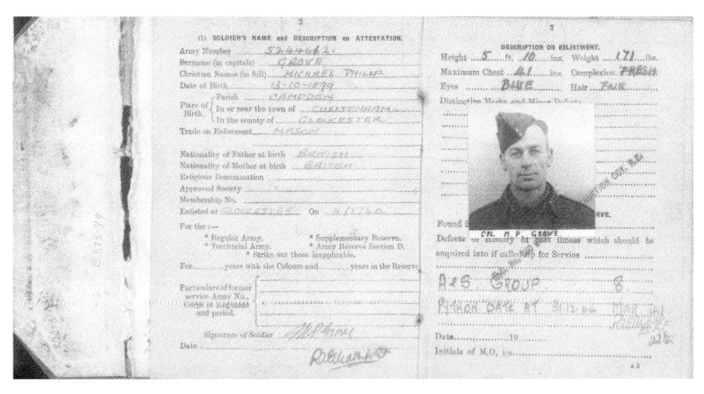

Paybook and Egyptian, Italian and Russian paper money

> **Camarades français!**
> Chaque heure de résistance inutile augmentera vos pertes.
> **Pour qui combattez-vous?**
> Il vaut mieux
> *vivre pour la France*
> que mourir pour l'Angleterre. Rendez-vous aux troupes allemandes, vous serez bien traités.
> **Cessez le feu!**

> **French fellows!**
> Every useless résistance hours will increase your losses
> **Who are you fighting for?**
> It will better:
> **To live for France**
> As die for England. Give you over to the German troops. You will be treated well
> **Hold the fire!**

German leaflet in French - English translation

The things I have written so far, are as near correct as I can make them. Sometimes a bit is in the wrong order and quite a bit not mentioned in case it becomes monotonous! I must add here though that about three days out to sea, coming home, I threw over the stern of the ship a beautiful Nine Millimetre Automatic pistol and four hundred rounds of ammunition. I do not know if I was stupid or not. You see I had carried them a long time but thought, if anyone's kit gets looked at during immigration inspection, it will be sure to be mine. That would be my luck, but as it happened, we were all formed up in lines, when we got off the ship, and the official just passed us all with no stoppage at all. One never knows, such a thing could have held me up or so I thought, perhaps it was for the best.

Before I leave the service altogether I feel I must go back and pick up a bit of information I missed out when we were on "Coal Island" in the River Shatt, at Basra. My OC asked me to do a couple of memorials to officers who had died at Basra. He said what they wanted and left me to it.

I did two concrete crosses set in heavy shaped plinths and with inscriptions cut in teak panels which I fixed as inserts into the plinths. They looked very good when I'd done.

One evening during the time I worked on these, our officers came up to our mess on a courtesy visit, (mostly to drink). The

OC asked me how I was getting on with the memorials. I told him, nearly ready, and went to my tent and brought out the two teak panels to show him the inscriptions, which I had already completed. He, and the others, were very pleased indeed. He said, "very beautifully carved Grove". But really they were a nice job, complete with Serifs nicely shaped. I had these jobs fixed up in the military cemetery at Basra.

There is one item I never mentioned, that is war medals. No value really, only sentimental. There are the three first war 1914-15 Star, General Service and Victory medals. There are my second war medals which I have never exposed or threaded on their appropriate ribbons.

Chapter Twenty Four
Settling back into Civilian Life

Now here I must settle down to civilian life and begin to earn my keep. Obviously it will be strange for a while, until I fit in. I thought that, as Arthur Pyment had passed on and also that as I had gained experience of Public Works in the Army, I would go to Pyments at the Guild and see if there was a possibility of getting engaged there, more in the managerial side of the trade. After all I had handled their best work before the war, but Harold did not seem very enthusiastic about it. Talked generally about things. Said he could retire even then. And in the end told me I could have my old job back. So I decided to leave it at that (although years later his wife remarked openly during a little party they gave, that Michael ought to have been there).

I went to work for a time with George Brotheridge and Co. Two farm cottages at Norton Grounds, then two pairs at Mickleton.

While this latter was going on there was a good deal of work to be done at Norton Hall. This property was then owned by Capt. Pollen. Brother Bob was already there as a semi invalid after a road smash near Troopers Lodge. I went and saw the people there and thought about it, and I had promised Brother Bob at Dunkirk that if we came through the War we would start a small business of our own.

Well in 1946 we did just that. To begin with, we rented a small area and sheds from Fred Keely, Coal Merchant, at the bottom of Hoo Lane. We used a home made hand cart for jobs around the town, and later purchased another slightly larger one which was professionally made. We progressed with mechanical transport, and also soon moved to larger premises, which was an enclosed yard area and farm buildings belonging to Miss Rimell at Wolds End. Although I worked very hard and looked out for jobs all the time, we never seemed to make any headway financially. Of course we may have been too painstaking with our work, or else not charged enough, on day work jobs. However it cannot now be helped.

We also took in brother Frank when he came home from war service, however he eventually left, and we paid him in full, having a special audit for it.

Anyway we progress and do some very good jobs about. Quite a few new houses and lots of alterations and modernising.

On a new house I built at Saintbury, I cut into the stone head over the front door, a compass and trowel. These were the trade symbols of the architect Tom Bateman, and myself, the mason, also both our initials and date.

My son Robert became a partner in the business and in a little while he dropped into full swing. My ancestors I know were in the trade, and I have traced us back to the 1600's. through the Church Register.

During recent years, Robert handled the building of the New Primary School, the new Clubroom etc. at the Royal British Legion, the general work connected with the Restoration of the Parish Church (we were the main contractors for that job). Also dealing with adjustments to all roof areas, including re-leading, refurbishment to all C.I. downpipes, and extensive work on the stone fabric.

He also is now dealing with the final part of the restoration of the Almshouses. This had been a very difficult job, full of problems, being the go between. Struggling with various sub contractors, materials being sent wrong and the eternal job of getting them straightened out. This kind of contract work has no financial reward, It's never paid for and inevitably ends in a loss.

Rob is in entire control of the business, has been now for the last seven years or so. Brother Bob retired some four years ago. I did in October 1967.

My last work was the repair and renewals of the Mullion Windows at the parish church during the Restoration 1968-71. I am well pleased and proud of the work which I did. I came out of retirement to carry out this work, and gave my time free of charge. Due to this my name is on a special lead panel with the other officials, which was fixed on to the new Lead of the Nave Roof by order of the committee. So my name is perpetuated as is the form.

Michael repairing stonework at St James' Church 1970
Also special lead panel on church roof

Also, in 1971, a party of the church officials arranged a gathering at "Grevel House". Present were Dr. Donald Olliff, Dr. Jennifer Olliff, Mr. and Mrs. Hargreaves-Beare, Col. Rose, the Vicar, The Rev. Peter White, and his Curate, my wife, and my sons and their wives; Tony and Jean and Robert and Betty.

During this gathering, Dr. Olliff presented me with a Silver Teapot. This was in recognition of my work on the Church. I was speechless, no words to say, but my feelings were high.

I was staggered by the gift, and very grateful to the donors. The Silver Teapot had been made at the Guild.

I have a few what I call souvenirs, some connected with my work. There is a sketch of the Church from the north east corner. I should say it was drawn from a point in "Parsons Close" signed and dated 1797 by the artist. It's not a good drawing but it shows what that side looked like at that time.

Old drawing, North Elevation St. James' Church
Dated 1797

Also I have a fine water-colour of the South East side of the Church which has plenty of details. No date or signature unfortunately. The painting is no doubt either a copy, or an impression, of a much earlier period. I think it could tie in with the date of the Standing Memorial inside the South-window of the Gainsborough Chapel. Now this painting shows it before the windows were made higher and before the battlements were raised, and it's obvious to me that the double windows in the chapel were made to show equal light on either side of the Memorial.

Water colour South East Elevation St. James' Church

I gave this window a lot of thought when I was working there, and decided that the window was put there before the Memorial, because it was finished on the inside, which could not have been done, with the Memorial in place, unless possibly the Memorial was moved, to do it? but again the height of the window clearly shows it. The memorial would never have stood in the recess as it would have been too tall.

Also I have a water colour of myself done on silk by a Chinese artist (cover picture). This was painted from a postcard photo taken about the end of the first war, and in the uniform I wore with Regimental Buttons and showing the 1914-15 Medal Ribbon, and the dandy cap I liked so much. (Brother Bill took this photo with him when he went on the China Station Service in the Royal Navy) and had it done there and brought safely back home. Probably painted at Shanghai.

There is a photo of my squad in the gym at Portsmouth during training.

Also somewhere there is an oil painting bust of me, painted by an Italian artist named Scarpenti, and done in the Refugee Camp on Kasos in 1945. [Both now lost. Ed.]

I have also a painted plaster cast of Sir Robert Dover's plaque given to me by Christopher Whitfield.

Robert Dovers Plaque built into stone pier on Dovers Hill

118

The plaque was made in the London Museum in stone, and which I fixed into a stone pillar on Dovers Hill. There may only be two or three of these casts in existence.

There is another water-colour of Leasebourne. This also is quite an old painting, as since then, big trees have grown all down Leasebourne. I remember there were one or two "plane" trees. They have all gone now, except the one near the Kettle. Note the man with the yoke on his shoulders, carrying two wooden buckets of water from the pump in the corner across the road, to the farm buildings behind the house. (Stamford House) He went through the Yard doors with the thatched roof over and up the back, where there were stables and cow sheds etc. I remember horses and carts, up and down there, and the rickyard was behind that, where the new houses are built in what is now called Marlands Close. (I remember threshing being done there). The man carrying the buckets was probably little Jimmy Howell or his father. The date probably anywhere at the end of the last century, I should say perhaps about 1890 or maybe be earlier.

Watercolour of Leasebourne showing Stamford House when in use as a farm

Mrs Margaret Wright brought me a large painting of the church as a token in respect of the service I gave concerning her house alteration and improvements at Greenstead Catbrook when she came to live there, and also as a slight reflection on my work at the church, and also for work that I did for her two sisters in law who lived next door, ex. nurse Wright and Mrs Molly Crick.

There is also a portrait in oils of my dear wife who was then about fourteen years old, painted by a very good artist who lived in a caravan for a long time around Campden. His name I have forgotten.

Painting of dear wife age 14

I have a few pieces of my stone carving, not good but for me full of sentiment.

Stone carvings by Michael

Probably himself    *Edith*    *Robert*

Stone carvings by Michael

Now I have come to the end of a useful working life and can look back over it all and wonder what might have been, but you know this century has been the most progressive of all. I have seen the first motor car, the first plane, Halley's Comet in 1910 and various flights to the moon. Oh yes it has certainly all happened in my life time, but now as I approach the age of seventy five, I can relax and enjoy the life which goes on all around me.

There are quite a few items, snaps and information which could well be transferred to the end of this story. Work reports, movement orders, list of the journey by road from Basra to Egypt etc.

The mine, Westington Quarry, Chipping Campden

Appendix
Thoughts on Local Stone

Throughout my working life, and as mentioned in my memoirs, I have spent most of that time working in stone, especially during the period 1924-1940. Fortunately stone was to be found in many places around Chipping Campden, and it had many variations in colour, texture and method of working.

The finest stone came from Westington Quarry, in early days this quarry was owned by the Lord of the Manor. Here the stone was mined and brought outside on a narrow rail track. It came out in large blocks and could then be chadded (split or chopped) to a desired size. This stone was clear and soft like butter, very soft to cut and easily roughly chopped to any given size. It was called free stone, and as it was so clear, was not easy to know face from bed. This is why I think that some of the flaking stone now showing in some old stone buildings is because they were what we call face bedded, meaning that in those cases, the stones were laid with their beds showing on face, which can then shale off particularly when affected by weathering conditions. In some cases, the only way to tell the difference was that the bed would be harder to cut than the face. All stone of course should be laid on its true bed, or as I would say, as it grew. It is also interesting to see the tiny shells and sand holes.

When stone is newly quarried, I found it needed to dry out some before being worked and carved succesfully.

Piscina in the beer cellar of Island Cellar
Photo taken by kind permission of the owner

123

I found if the stone was new and still wet, it would stick to the chisel, and bits just pluck off, so in practice I always made sure that the stone was well dry before carving, also the dust cleans out easily.

Incidently George Tap, a quarry worker, was killed when a stone fell out of the roof of the mine, this was about 1909 or thereabouts, and I don't think the mine was worked much after that time, but I am not quite sure about this.

When you look around the buildings in Campden, there are instances where stone from other areas has been added here and there. Generally as it weathered down it was not very noticable, but becomes more evident on buildings when they have been cleaned by washing down, at this time the darker colour, usually pieces of Coscombe stone then stands out like a sore thumb.

I reckon our stone is the Queen of the Cotswolds. As one travels further south, the stone becomes greyer and colder looking. I was never a lover of Bath stone, I thought it to be too soft and not hold its edges. Now Portland stone I have worked with a lot, it's very good, holds up well and weathers well, but again so cold and harsh looking. I remember the "Obelisk" I did in Mansfield stone, this is a very hard sandstone, and I found that it was neccessary to sharpen my tools about every two letters.

The stone for ordinary building work, (not ashlar face) was dug out from the open quarry face. It would be stacked in cubic

Stone mullion window in garden wall of Darby House
Photo taken by kind permission of the owner

yards made up of various height stones, and sold by the cubic yard. Many years ago dry stone walling was carried out to form boundaries of properties, and also a general form of field fencing. This was especially so up on the hills where stone could be readily found close to hand.

Blocked up window, Town Hall north elevation
Photo taken by kind permission of the owner

Small quarry holes were quite common around the area. Dry stone walls were built slightly tapered, and about three foot high with coomers set on top which helped to give the wall added strength, and bound the top together. During the building, long stones were laid that went right through the wall and projected a few inches on each side, this helped strengthen the wall, but also made points where one could easily climb over without doing damage. These walls of course gave exellent protection for sheep, where they could find shelter from the wind and rain, but especially snow, winter conditions in the Cotswolds have been known to be very severe. Also repairs to these walls gave work for men in the quiet countryside, as in these times in these rural areas, there was very little work about, and labour was very cheap.

In the distant past, stone slates were produced in abundance, they came from quarries where the stone was hard, and in layers of very thin beds. The stone would be quarried and stood on end where the rain and frost would split open the beds, they would then be dressed to size, and holed ready for fixing, all this work done by hand. Stone slate roofing was interesting work, the slates were hung over the battens using hand made oak

Well in beer cellar of Island Cellar
Photo taken by kind permission of the owner

pegs fixed into the slate holes, and the laps carefully worked out. Originally each different length of slate had its own special name. There being no underfelt in those times, the underside of the slates were always "torched" with lime mortar in order to keep out the draught. After a number of years, the "torching" would begin to perish and parts would become detached leaving gaps, and in blizzard conditions snow would blow through the gaps and pile up inside the roof space. In those instances it was neccessary to gain access into the roof space, and remove the snow, usually by bucket, before it melted and ran through the bedroom ceiling.

Now as I walk in Campden's high street, my past thoughts on the Town Hall and The Island Cellar return. Although there seems to be no knowledge that the Town Hall was ever a church, certain facts prove otherwise? Look at the buttresses on the front elevation, and the blocked up windows on the north side, also on this same elevation, one can see what appears to be a blocked up doorway which is quite wide, and also very low, which suggests that in the past, the roadway could have been a lot lower. Also built into a garden wall at Darby house is what I believe to be a fourteen century stone mullion church window, reputed to have been taken out of the Town Hall? I further believe that The Island Cellar may be built on what was once a Chapel. In the base of the building, now used as a beer cellar, there are niches in the walls, and also a "Piscina". There is also a blocked up doorway which may have been an underground passage leading to the present Town Hall. A well is also in existence. It would be good if a historian could research these buildings, as far too much local history is lost to us.

Coram   Deo   Laboramus

"Let us work in the presence of God"

Michael Grove aged 79 on the Cotswold Way 1979